Journey of an

Empath

A collection of personal stories from

Empaths around the world

Printed in Australia
First Printing, 2018
ISBN: 978-0-6482128-2-9
White Light Publishing House
Hillside, VIC, Australia 3037

whitelightpublishing.com.au

White Light
PUBLISHING HOUSE

Highly sensitive people are too often perceived as weaklings or damaged goods. To feel intensely is not a symptom of weakness, it is the trademark of the truly alive and compassionate. It is not the empath who is broken, it is society that has become dysfunctional and emotionally disabled. There is no shame in expressing your authentic feelings. Those who are at times described as being a 'hot mess' or having 'too many issues' are the very fabric of what keeps the dream alive for a more caring, humane world. Never be ashamed to let your tears shine a light in this world.

Anthon St. Maarten

Introduction

If you've picked up this book, it's likely you at least have some understanding of the term, 'Empath' and are either wanting to know more about it for yourself or for someone you love. Let us clear up what it means to be an empath, to begin with.

Being **empathetic** is not an unusual thing. Most humans have empathy. It means that you can relate to what someone else may be feeling, putting yourself in someone else's shoes in a situation (for example, if a friend is nervous about standing up in front of a group people, you might recall what that felt like when you had to do the same thing, and so you empathise with them).

Being **empathic** on the other hand, is being a highly sensitive person who can deeply perceive emotions of others and feel what they feel. An empath tunes in to others' emotions and energy intuitively – without even trying. Being empathic is like being a magnet. You attract the energy and emotions of people, places, situations to you, and you absorb it all as your own. And, you don't even need to be in the same vicinity to do so.

This book contains a collection of personal stories from empaths around the world, who have experienced both the challenges and the rewards of this amazing gift. If you're an empath yourself, or know someone who is, you will not at all be surprised if you find yourself having quite a few 'aha' moments throughout this book, as well as learning something new along the way.

As with any person, each of our journeys are unique, as you'll find throughout the words on these pages. What you will discover however, is that empaths do share many things in common – and it's these qualities and gifts that are going to help change the future of humanity as we know it.

Namaste, and I hope that through reading these stories, that you come away feeling more empowered and loved than you were before.

Christie

Dedicated to all those empaths who did not have the strength
to complete their journeys here on earth this time around.

Message from
Archangel Metatron

Channeled through Sharon Miralles

Archangel Metatron oversees all sensitive souls and empaths. He helps all those who are called to the path of service, illuminating their path, providing guidance, support, comfort and healing. With his Light energy and spiritual, esoteric teachings and wisdom, he is the perfect, Divine ally to assist all empaths as they embrace their sacred gifts and walk the path of Light.

Archangel Metatron brings you this message. May it touch your Light within and may you feel it deep within your soul, assisting you to know that your empathic gifts are normal, inherent and what all humans are capable of experiencing - of Being. It is your true soul essence.

I bring comfort to you empathic souls to lighten your load and encourage you to share your gifts wisely with others. First and foremost, your feeling nature is designed to be of service and sustenance for your soul. It offers you an awakened truth and ability to discern for yourself truth always. This inner truth awareness allows you to know which path to take always and beacons for you to follow it always. This gift may seem overwhelming at times, but you are custodians of sacred knowledge that when harnessed properly, becomes wisdom - Divine spiritual wisdom that transcends all time and space and human conditioning. Your innate soul essence is wise, compassionate, empathetic, all-knowing, all-feeling, telepathic and would never harm another soul. When you awaken your full empathic capabilities, you are living from your true soul essence. This is who you are. Not your body. Not your mind. Your soul. Be empathic. Embrace your calling and your Light. Serve others with the gifts your Creator has bequest you. Be truth, be Light, be One.

I await your call and I shall be in loving service,

Metatron

With love, light and unity,

Sharon Miralles

Contents

The Secret of the Soul

Ann Hannon Hughes

The gift of empathy, together with so many spiritual gifts, is packed away in our soul, bestowed upon us when we made our journey from Divine Consciousness - from where we all came - to our chosen experience of being human. Collectively, these tools, like a compass, are used to guide and help us along our journey through life, with all its dark caves and mesmerising mountain peaks, enabling us to find our way and remember who we are and in which direction we are going. We are all spiritual beings having a human experience.

Our human body grows, ages and dies, but our spirit never dies, and once released from the confines of the limitations of a human body, it returns to the loving creator energy of source. How easy life would be if we knew from the beginning that we had such tools and could access them as and when needed, but it doesn't work like that. As soon as we are born into our human bodies, we forget where we came from and that we have our own spiritual compass within. This is the secret of the soul. Life is like a quest of self-discovery; a journey of experiences through choices, finding and using our spiritual gifts along the way and ultimately returning to the source of all that is, the Divine Consciousness, the Creator, God or whatever loving name we attribute it.

The gift of empathy is our spiritual antenna, connecting us back to source and to every other human being. It is our spiritual gift of 'feeling', which is how empathy connects. To be conscious of your own, and everyone else's energy; to be connected to the loving creator energy of source; to be able to feel all the wonderful experiences and feelings of others, your environment, and mother earth, must be the most uplifting and magical gift to be bestowed upon you, right? Not always! Agreed, it is amazing and definitely assists in our moving forward with our personal spiritual growth and transformation, but it can be painful, too. This is the gift of being an Empath.

Although most of us grow up unaware of our spiritual gift of empathy, we may notice our sensitiveness to people and places around us. We 'feel' uncomfortable or lifted in certain places or in the company of certain people. We may not know what it actually is and may just sense that there's an 'atmosphere' around a place or person. I have always had these sensitivities; picking up on bad vibes and avoiding situations and people who I believed were not good for me, or honing in on people or places with good vibes, but I believed it was just part of me being aware and nothing to do with anything spiritual. I certainly didn't see my being sensitive as a gift or wisdom, which it truly is. My spiritual quest began during my late teens/early twenties, but my being sensitive to places and people has been with me for as long as I can remember.

To be sitting in a park quietly, minding your own business and listening to the peaceful sounds of nature; to then suddenly be overcome with feelings of uncertainty or nervousness, for no known or apparent reason. You feel restless all of a sudden, so you move from your place, on instinct, more than a planned conscious move. As you move away, your feelings may fade or indeed strengthen, depending on which direction you move. Instinctively, you move in a direction that lessens your negative feelings until you feel safe and grounded again. This whole experience is carried out without seeing anything that could have threatened your peace like that, but you knew on a deeper level that you were uncomfortable and felt the need to move out of that discomfort. This is empathy.

You might call it intuition, gut feeling, a hunch etc. and that is perfect and true, but empathy is the spiritual gift of 'all feeling' and is your connection to the all-that-is loving source, and to every other living thing on earth. Those feelings you have, without known cause, are a reminder of such connection.

You may never know what happened in the park that day that made you feel so uncomfortable, but had you remained, you would probably have found that something would have happened that wouldn't have been favourable for you. There could have been a wild dog lurking nearby ready to pounce and attack you in some harmful way. Or, there may have been a group of unruly teens making their way towards you, who may have teased you or even worse. It doesn't really matter what the event, you 'felt' and 'knew' beforehand that the positive energy had changed around you and your feelings told you it was time to move.

I am reminded of a time when I lived in England returning home from work one evening. It was winter time and at 6.00 pm, it was dark and drizzly as I got off my bus to walk the seven or so minutes' journey to my front door. Although I did this every evening, one night as I turned the corner from the main road into my avenue, I had an uneasy feeling. I continued walking but quickened my pace, thinking that someone may be behind me. After a minute or two I turned around, but there was no one there. I continued walking along the darkened tree-lined avenue, lit up sporadically by dimmed lamp posts. Those feelings made me think that my otherwise very pretty avenue was quite creepy in the darkness and I put my feelings down to that and shrugged them off.

Then, I heard a shrill. I'd never heard anything like it before, or indeed since. It came from out of the darkness ahead of me and I stopped in my tracks. I felt weak and frightened, and my legs turned to jelly. I had to lean against the garden wall of a house beside me in order to stay upright. Almost immediately, there was a second noise and this time it was a high-pitched scream. As if all happening at once, a lady ran out of her house from across the road and straight over to me, asking whether I was alright. I can't remember what I blubbered from my mouth, but she said she had heard the scream and thought something had happened to me. Immediately, a man came running towards us out of the darkness asking if anyone had passed, as a girl had just been attacked further down the avenue and the perpetrator ran off once the neighbours rushed out of their homes upon hearing the scream. We didn't see anyone else and apparently the assailant got away. The girl survived what could have been a far more serious attack, thanks to the quick actions of a few neighbours who heard her screams.

I tell this story to highlight my own feelings as I turned into the avenue that evening. I felt all was not well but had put it down to the darkness of the avenue unnerving me and nothing else. Had I been conscious of being empathic and how it works for me, I would have known I was walking into a negative situation and may have prepared myself differently, as opposed to just brushing the feeling off and being crippled by shock and fear upon hearing that shrill. I might have known if those awful feelings were my own or those of the girl in front of me. I will never know for sure, but I do believe I would have acted differently once wisdom was on my side. The wisdom that accompanies 'feeling' in the gift of being an empath is 'knowing'.

It is my experience that empathy, although a feeling gift, comes hand in hand with the gift of knowing. I see it as feeling is of the heart and knowing is of the mind. The knowing part of empathy lets me know on a deeper level what my feelings are telling me. For instance, if there is a negative feel around me I can more often than not, know whether it is my own energy or that of someone else. It may seem obvious that we would know where our feelings stem, but I believe unless we are truly conscious to the gift of empathy, we tend to claim all feelings as our own, but this is not always the case. Knowing is what helps us distinguish the line between ourselves and others, or between two different emotions. Knowing, if you like, are clues we receive to help us trace, assess and deal with the feelings we are experiencing. If the person in the park was aware of their empathy they would probably have taken the same action, but rather than on raw instinct, they would have known on a deeper level that there was danger and they were to move away.

Over the years, I have learned the true benefits of the gift of empathy. Regardless of what it assists us with in terms of daily life, it is first and foremost a spiritual tool of connection. To be connected through the spiritual energy of every living thing, and knowing all beings have this energy connection from the divine loving source energy of consciousness itself, reminds us of something we had forgotten since birth, but has always been part of us. This is the gift of connection; a connection that can be felt. Different people use their gift of empathy in different ways, but for me, my greatest service with empathy is in the connection with others who are hurting. This is something I couldn't do of course until I had experienced pain myself.

Pain has shown itself to me on many occasions during my life, but none as strong as the pain of grief. Loss of loved ones throws us into the depths of spiritual pain with the most painful part being the pain of disconnection. The disconnection from our loved one leaves us with feelings of solitude, helplessness and above all, a broken heart. A heart that grows cold because the love of another has stopped warming it; a heart missing from this world that doesn't require your love anymore; these are the irrational and yet real feelings of the pain of disconnection. These feelings plunge us deeper and deeper into the abyss until such time there is nothing. Nothing to love, nothing to touch, nothing to feel and nothing to see. It is then in the thick murky energy of darkness, while gasping for air, that a spark of light appears.

This spark of light reminds us that we are more than our human experience. It reminds us that we are never alone, and it has come to assist us in lifting ourselves one step at a time, from the murky nothingness of grief.

As we slowly rise again, the light expands little by little, reminding us of the gifts we hold inside; of our soul purpose and the power of our life experiences. A dark night of the soul is probably the most powerful experience we will go through as a human being. One doesn't have to lose loved ones to enter this spiritual night, but regardless of which situation is the cause, the feelings of hopelessness, loss and nothingness will be the same.

Our spiritual gifts remind us of how capable and powerful we are once we understand that we are spiritual beings first. They don't ever stop teaching us and there is no end point of "I'm there". Even after death when, I believe, we look back and assess our lives and how we used our gifts, we will come to understand from that viewpoint, that we could have grown more into our gifts.

Once we tap into the true gift of empathy, we are not just acting instinctively, but we gain wisdom through knowing around our feelings and can gain more control over what we do with those feelings. The more we work with this gift, the more we open up to the wisdom provided to us by the loving creator of all that is.

Since waking up to my own gift of empathy I have still had experiences in some ways similar to the one I had walking home after work on that winter's night, but with the awareness of knowing I was being warned, I consciously changed my behaviour to move me away from any negative impact that such events may have caused me.

Through my own journey of healing and transformation, I have met and connected with others who have suffered deep and personal pain. I have found that through my empathic gift, I have felt their pain and been able to guide them back towards hope. As my own empathic gift of feeling expands, so too does its partner gift of knowing, and this has helped me recognise - both in myself and others - clues that can help trace back to the root of unhappiness. From the deep depression of grief, to the everyday challenges of coping with life, I can tap into the energy surrounding someone and identify the root feeling that other feelings stem from. Loss, for instance, has a common set of feelings, whether the person has lost a loved one, a friendship, a job, or even a precious belonging. If that loss has hurt them deeply, their energy will emit a feeling of 'loss'. It wouldn't really matter what the circumstances are, but I would feel their feelings of loss and encourage them to identify, own and heal such emotional pain.

I also find that people tend to feel embarrassed when they suffer pain of loss over say, a job or a pet that has gone missing, as if it is something that shouldn't be felt as pain. These people would tend to say they are fine and pass their circumstance off as "just the way it is, I'll get over it". On a number of occasions, I have told people that I can feel their hurt and it is perfectly acceptable to feel such pain over any type of loss. People tend to feel guilty, like their loss isn't big enough to hurt. My advice is to feel your pain and face it, as it may be a spiritual lesson on the experience of loss, and if it doesn't grab your attention this time around it may well come calling again, but a bit louder. I find this is the way with spiritual lessons.

I remember just the other week, shopping in our local supermarket and looking through their gluten free products. I was just browsing the different labels and a young girl was standing next to me. She asked if I was a celiac and I told her that my daughter was, and I started to talk about the expense of a gluten free diet. She said she was also a celiac and that she tried to shop cheaply for gluten free foods, but sometimes would eat non-gluten free foods because of cost. I sympathised with her that she had to eat food that could be damaging her health because of cost and carried on with my browsing. I then felt her energy; I picked up on a sadness of loss and knew she wanted to talk so I turned to her again and just asked, "are you okay?" She said, "not really" and proceeded to talk to me about her being alone with a little boy to care for. She talked about her little boy loving school and how they have a dog who the boy loves. To me, it was simple everyday chat with a stranger, who was understandably finding it difficult as a lone parent, but I still felt energy around her of loss. After a couple of minutes chatting, she then told me that she had recently lost her job and that was why she was struggling to make ends meet. I again sympathised and was asking about her work and suggested that she register straight away for support and start looking for further work with the appropriate agencies. She told me she had done all this and in fact was quite positive that something would turn up for her. But, her words weren't matching her energy, so I told her that I was getting the impression she was upset about something.

This is when she told me that she shouldn't have lost her job, as she was there longer than people who remained and she believed that one particular person had taken over her work who wasn't as qualified as she. Once she told me this part of her situation, I knew it to be true as it resonated with the energy I was feeling. The pain she felt was from her colleague's perceived betrayal and this also impacted her personal self-esteem. We chatted for another while and I explained a few things and how I saw them and offered suggestions of how she could help herself deal with her feelings of loss and betrayal. Eventually, she seemed to perk up, thanked me for talking to her and carried on her way.

This is typical of people who feel down or sad, but do not value their own feelings and self-worth. They tend to hide their true feelings as they figure their problem isn't 'big enough' to feel pain. I think this is a common problem in the world today and people need to know that we all matter, our feelings matter, and that pain is pain, regardless of its level.

Children, I believe, are more in tune with their empathic feelings and there is an honesty about them that is truthful, magical and wonderful. In my opinion, their human conditioning hasn't impacted them for long enough to close down their openness and free-spirited essence of connection. I found that once becoming a mom, my empathy deepened and being in tune with the energy of my children was definitely helpful. I believe all mothers have this deep empathy with their children, and I also believe the parent/child spiritual connection is one of the easiest to fine tune. Through empathic connection with my children, I have discovered truths I may not have otherwise known, dealt with illness before symptoms appeared, felt their sadness and concerns when attempts were made to keep them hidden, celebrated their feelings of achievement at the smallest of things; the things adults wouldn't usually recognise as being the 'big things', and so much more. I am sure all or most parents reading this will be nodding in agreement.

During my time working with children, the energy around them was so light and uplifting that everyone - children and staff alike - seemed to benefit energetically from just their presence. When I worked in the school environment, there were a few children who were deeply sensitive with their personalities coming across as 'shy'. I noted that within this group of children, there were two distinct types. There was the quiet child who preferred to be alone and seemed happy and content in their own company, but there was another type of child who although appeared shy, I felt they wanted to be part of the collective, but were reluctant and held themselves back from joining in. With both types of children, I would encourage them to join in the play and activities with their friends, but I found the few who were happy on their own wouldn't attempt to try to join in or might have stepped forward but remained quiet and wouldn't mix. However, the majority of the reluctant group, when encouraged and accompanied, would move forward into the bigger group and happily join in when invited.

I believe this second type of child is more in touch with their feelings of empathy and their antenna are perhaps just picking up on the boisterous or energetically charged feelings of the other children, and not knowing how to interpret these, so felt pushed back from joining in. We must be so observant of the children in our care that we never overlook their sensitivities around feelings, as I believe to miss the opportunity of teaching them about the gift of feeling, could be detrimental to their spiritual wellbeing as they grow up. We should be slow to label children as 'shy' and should always try to bring out their playful and sociable nature in a gentle and understanding way, before accepting that a child is happier in their own company.

There are times when interactions with people can tire me. I believe that when we connect with others empathically, we sometimes retain traces of their energy within our own energy field. For me, I find myself thinking about a certain person's troubles long after we parted company and I know I have picked up some of their energy and brought it home with me. When this happens, I rest. It's that simple. I have learned, over time, there are situations I should avoid. Crowded places tire me so much and I could get feelings of heaviness or indeed hyper-wired, which leave me feeling overwhelmed and empty, or fired up. Funeral gatherings leave me feeling physically sick and I avoid them as best I can, preferring to pass my condolences privately at another time. But, rest is the antidote for any such feelings of negative energy. I love my 'alone time', being in touch with my own feelings and my connection to the divine source and I make time every day where I can shut out the world and rejuvenate my energy batteries. I thank God, every evening for the day he gave me, with its lessons and blessings, and I fall asleep at peace. The following day upon waking, I give thanks for another day where I may make a difference, or to just experience what it is to be me.

I would encourage everyone to discover their gift of empathy. Next time you get a hunch, a vibe, or a piece of intuition, feel where it comes from. Become conscious of which part of your body is feeling this. If you are on a spiritual path, acknowledge this as part of your gift of empathy and ask the divine source to guide you to 'knowing'. Empathy is a gift to us all and all we need is to acknowledge it and work with our feelings more, and it will grow and reveal itself to us in the best way possible.

To feel loved by God, the divine source of all that is, and to be able to connect with others through that love, is the most powerful and loving thing we can do for ourselves and others. In imagining a place full of empathic understanding and healing our feelings of disconnection, one can truly envision a more compassionate and peaceful world.

Our feelings are real, our feelings matter, and they are part of our divine gift of empathy.

In love and light,

Ann

Survival, Hope & Healing

Belinda Hayes – The Spiritual Teacher

One of the hardest things I have had to come to terms with, being an empath, is my depth of feelings. The ability to be 'empathetic' is used a lot in psychology and counselling, or any other human service role, but it is described as the ability to connect into the emotion of another person (usually one that is being treated or healed) without becoming engaged in their emotion. It is defined as the ability to be able to stand aside from it while still being present. To acknowledge the emotion in which that person is feeling, without taking it on board.

So, am I *empathetic*? No, because, very rarely do I not feel the emotion myself. Very rarely can I sit beside a person whose energy is absorbed as deeply in an emotion, such as grief, and not feel that same depth of grief as they do. What I am, is clairsentient; an **empath**. And, as an empath, I *feel* - deeply.

As an empath, my journey has been a remarkable one; one that has required a depth of conviction, deep understanding and continued growth, as well as a learned education in what I was feeling and if those feelings were mine or others. A personal schooling on how to recognise the signs, shapes, colours and feelings of energy and the means to engage in the world around me as a normal, functional being without being absorbed by that energy.

I first knew and understood that I processed the world differently, at a very young age. Growing up, I thought that everyone was feeling what I was; struggling to understand the world around them, as I was, and that they were as emotional and intrigued by the world and its events as I was. But that was not the case. Instead, as a child, I was often being told I was 'soft' and 'a bleeding heart'. I was told 'to harden up' and 'stop carrying on'. I was constantly criticised by those around me when I reacted or responded to events and stimuli differently to the way they did, and I was so, so confused by it all.

I had the hardest time understanding why everyone else around me wasn't in tears at the World Vision ads on TV showing the small African children starving, or why when Robin Williams died, everyone else was not grieving like I was? How they could walk past a homeless person in the streets and not stop to ask them how they were and offer them food, or how they would not feel physically ill at the sight of a bear in a cage being used for the extraction of bile. Around me, I saw the world, and I connected with it. I felt its energy and I wept. I struggled, and I mourned. Yes, I was empathetic to the goings on around me, but I was not aside from it, I was part of it – it was part of me.

I grew up struggling with how to cope with the depth of what I felt and the confliction of my emotions that would rise up randomly, as I brushed passed people and entered into their auric field. I struggled with the emotion of the world more than others seemed to, and as a result I hated the world around me. I found it cruel and impractical. I found it hateful and beautiful at the same time. I found joy and sorrow in the same space and in an effort to try to find my place in the world - I rebelled against it; *hard*!

I tried to block out my emotions (or the emotions of others that I too, felt) however I couldn't, so I searched for other like-minded souls - friends like me - to help guide me and give me answers, but I never truly found any. As a child, I found I was unable to express myself, but I could feel everything. I was unable to control these feelings and instead I overacted or shut down. Unsure what life was all about and not sure if one emotion connected to the next, or if they were all meant to exist together like they were? I was lost and scared, unsure and alone.

Sadly (yet importantly), I think there are many children in the world today that are afflicted with the same desire to understand what they are feeling, as I was.

As the world begins to awaken on a greater scale, more and more children are being born into the world sensitive to energies and emotions. Aware of their existence and the universal life force energy and, they too, are going through the struggle to understand what it means to be an empath; to be clairsentient. That is why sharing my story and my journey is so important to me.

I was ten years old before I truly began to understand that I was connected to a greater energy than most. I felt things that others didn't, but more than that – I saw and heard things too, that others didn't. It was at this age I first met 'Grand-Poppy'. I was away for the school holidays with my best friend and her family, at a holiday destination on the Queensland Coast. Her family had rented an old holiday house and on the day we arrived, there was a gentleman that I saw residing in the house with us in one of the spare rooms. He was an older man, appearing in his late seventies, with greying hair and a scruffy grey beard. He wore dark blue fisherman overalls and a plain red baseball cap. He was friendly and smiled at me when I first saw him. He tipped his hat at me and introduced himself. He told me there was great fishing around these areas and to enjoy my holiday.

Grand-Poppy would always give me that same friendly smile whenever I saw him heading outside, or when I passed his room. I truly believed he was a guest in the house too. It was not until my friend and I passed him one day in the hallway of the holiday home and I smiled and said 'hello' to him, that my friend looked at me quizzically, asking me who on Earth I was talking to. I casually tilted my head in his direction and replied, "Grand-Poppy". She looked at me like I was mad and laughed out loud at me, asking me just who Grand-Poppy was. It was at that moment that I realised that she could not see him - only I could.

It turned out that Grand-Poppy used to reside in the home and had passed away many, many decades earlier. He was an elderly fisherman who always wore overalls. He was well loved by the local children who always affectionately referred to him as 'Grand-Poppy'. After learning this, it was with fear and incredulousness that I approached the next few days, unsure of whether I had seen a ghost or if my friend was just unable to see 'people' the way I did. Was I different, or was she? And if it was me that was different, then why and what did it all mean? I was to find out two weeks after this appearance by this grandfatherly spirit to me, of the significance of that event. And, it would haunt me for the rest of my life.

Shortly after seeing 'Grand-poppy', I was sexually assaulted by my own Earthly grandfather and a period of deep seeded trauma (that spirit would later assist me in healing) was implanted within my soul and my own spiritual energy. But, more importantly, I had my first ever answer as to why Grand-Poppy appeared to me – but the answer was not one that I would hear or understand for almost two and a half decades later.

My second major answer to life's mysteries came to me at the age of just fourteen years. A school friend was having a sleepover at my home and in the middle of the night we decided to sneak outside to have a midnight swim in our backyard pool. It was pitch black outside and as we did not want to wake my parents up and alert them to our mischievousness, we had not turned on any of the pool or outside lights. I was in the shallow end of the pool, just standing and talking to my friend, when she suddenly called out to me, asking me who I was talking to, after surfacing in the deep-end. When I looked back, there was a young girl standing in the pool next to me, around my age (14-16 years old), that I had been talking to. By the time I realised and looked back to where my friend was at the other end of the pool, the spirit I had been talking to had disappeared. That night, as we slept, each and every poster that I had hanging on my walls and back of my doors showing images of the famous idols of the time (such as Keanu Reeves, Jonathan Brandis or JTT) were all removed off my walls and stuck on top of each other, creating one single pile of posters. Neither one of us could have done this without waking the other up, by standing on their bed and heads to get to each poster. This was the first poltergeist-like activity I had experienced and was unexplainable at the time.

Then, three weeks after this incident, I was attacked in the local park by a gang of girls my own age and beaten up quite badly (all over a teenage boy). Piece number two of the puzzle was offered to me again by spirit as an advanced warning of who and what, but I was not able to understand or hear the message at that time. Instead, I began to feel a deep sense of dread at the appearance of spirit in my life.

It was not until I was sixteen years of age that I started to truly understand the apparitions as warnings that spirit was trying to offer me. It was a Saturday evening and I was in my bedroom with my boyfriend when quite suddenly, the lamp on my bedside table began to turn on and off again, repeatedly. This lamp was a gold nineties touch lamp (the type that uses your own personal electrical impulses to turn on and off, with each touch making the illumination brighter and brighter, cycling through before finally turning off again). However, instead of cycling through, the lamp continued to turn on and then directly off, repeatedly. My boyfriend, concerned that the house was experiencing an electrical surge, reached down to unplug the lamp from the wall, only to pick up the plug from the ground after finding it was not even plugged in. As he held the unplugged cord in his hand, the lamp once again turned on and then off – resulting in him throwing the cord to the ground and running from my room. Sighing, I sat down on my bed, only to have the doona beside me indent as an unseen entity sat down beside me. I knew what was coming, as by now I recognised the signs and that very night an intruder broke into my home, entering through my window, hiding under my bed and sexually attacking me. He took my innocence and sense of security and safety after dark, once the lights were turned out, just as I was being warned.

It did not take long for a broken, sad and desperately lonely sixteen-year-old to soon begin associating spirit *with* trauma. Eventually, any sighting, any whisper, any feeling, or any touch by them sent me into a rebellious rage that saw me fight back and refuse to allow them to enter my space, for fear of the event that would unfold following a message from them. I blamed them for the trauma I suffered in my life and because of my child-like understanding of the world, I began to dismiss them. I stepped fully back into my ego, living through my amygdala and no longer through my pineal gland. I lived for the next twenty years in survival mode, rather than in a space of unconditional love and intuition.

Of course, as you can expect, this threw me into a deep sense of loneliness and despair as I had forever sensed, seen, heard and connected with spirit and it felt as if I had lost a part of 'me'. As the years wore on, I rebelled even more, trying to find what I was missing. I was an all feeling, lonely, lost soul and I had no idea why. It was not until 2008 when I met some of my first mentors within the spiritual industry that I first started to see and understand the world for the very first time.

I began to understand the energy around me and the effect it had on me, and I began to breathe again. I began to gain a sense of purpose.

Around this time, a TV series had come on the air, called, 'The One'. It was a program designed to showcase psychic abilities, eliminating a contestant each week until a winner was announced. I would sit transfixed to this show, feeling a connection to the psychics and mediums and receiving my own messages as they aired different places, people and things. I sat enthralled as Mitchell Coombes made the first exit and sat mesmerized as Charmaine Wilson searched for information on the Peter Falconio case in the Season One finale. I watched Maria Elita, Julie McKenzie, Stacie De Marco & Michael Wheeler move through the second series and I began to realise something. These were the friends; the people I had been searching for. These were the like-minded souls I craved to find in my youth.

After watching this show, I made a conscious effort to personally connect with them all. I met Charmaine in person at a local event she was hosting. I had a crystal bed healing by Maria in her first ever healing centre in Brisbane, Queensland and I booked a reading with Michael over the phone and heard what he had to say. One thing I noticed throughout each meeting was that all of them mentioned my amazing ability to feel energy. All of them talked of the world of light-workers and my role within this light-worker's world. All of them saw into my soul and saw **me**! More importantly, they understood me, embraced me for it and they knew me better than I knew myself.

It was as a result of this, in 2008, that one of these beautiful souls gave me the name of my first Reiki Master and through being attuned to the energy of Reiki, I truly felt the power of my connection with spirit once more. By then, I was twenty-seven years old and still searching – despite being now married and planning children. Over the years in between, I had travelled the world and even bought my first home and while I did not know it yet, I was about to become a carer for my mother full-time for the next three years (as she would spiral into PTSD and severe anxiety and depression following my parent's divorce after thirty-two years of marriage). Again, despite my rejection of them over a decade earlier, spirit had led me to where I was needed and had helped me to find a part of me that I was craving. They had ensured I had the support I needed to endure what I was about to endure then and overcome the further trauma that I was yet to experience in my adult life.

As an adult, especially one connected to the life force energy that Reiki provided me, I began to see the world through a different lens.

I began to manifest to me the things that I wanted and needed in my life and more importantly, I began to attract around me my soul tribe. The people that would lead me on my journey into the empathic world; into the world of light-workers. The Earthly people that would guide me through my own awakening. I would also attract to me though, those that saw my light and craved what I had. Those that used people's energy to their own benefit. Those that succeeded only by bringing down those around them. We all know them; they are the narcissists of this world. The draggers. The pullers. They are the ones that see the soul of another and use it to their own advantage, and of course, as an empath and a clairsentient, we gravitate towards these people as their auras and energetic fields scream for help, attention and love.

It was in 2013 that I first met the narcissist that would lead to my final and eventual awakening. The one that would take me to the brink of the veil of this world and allow me to find the inner stillness of myself and my mind. The one that would force me to stop and take check of my life and my value and fill my world and its surroundings with unconditional love and healing. He was the catalyst to my spiritual journey and embarkation as it exists today and was the culmination of decades of guidance, love, support and protection from the spiritual world. For that, I will always be thankful to him (as it is only through gratitude that we fully encounter the world).

As I mentioned, since completing my Reiki course in 2008, I had been told over and over again that I had become a great manifestor. I had this amazing ability to create things in my life and to attract to me whatever it was that I asked for or wanted. Some have even viewed my life as easy and 'served up to me'. A sentiment I could never understand, considering the trauma I have suffered and the bloody hard work that I have put into making my life what it is today - but I learned, that they are right! I do manifest well. I can get anything I want. I can make it happen! Manifestation is one thing; a true awakening though, comes through an understanding of energy and of love, and I was to learn that lesson completely only three years ago, in 2015.

Let me take you back into the middle of 2015 and the end of my relationship with the aforementioned narcissist. I was the owner of a brand new and successful business in Brisbane, having literally built it from the ground up after investing everything I had into it. I had eleven staff employed within the business and I was the Managing Director. Simultaneously, I was also the joint shareholder of a blue-collar company (that my new partner had started with a loan of start-up money from me). Our company employed over seven contractors with contracts on multi-million-dollar home refurbishments and new home builds in new estates. At home, I had a new partner of two years and my divorce had just been finalised. His stepson was the third child that I had always wanted, and I thought that life was perfect. It was busy - very, very busy - and I spent up to sixteen hours per day working, but I loved it! So, despite my childhood trauma and the journey I had been on, I had worked hard, and I was doing really well for myself and my children. I had a relationship, multiple business endeavours, and life (albeit busy), was wonderful.

That was, until the night that that my partner and I fought, and it resulted with me laying in a hospital bed with my head split open to the skull and a possible fractured eye socket. As the doctor took my hand and asked me if I was safe and whether he wanted me to call the police, I suddenly realised that I was living in a home of domestic abuse and violence. I was being subjected to narcissistic love and my life was NOT perfect and I was NOT happy. I was in fact, busy - too busy to realise what my soul was trying to tell me. Too busy to realise that my energy was drained and that I was slowly dying from the inside out. I had lost 'me' and who I really was. I had lost the essence of myself, an essence that I lost somewhere around the age of sixteen and never truly found again. An essence that I wanted badly to find once more and that my tribe and the like-minded souls within the light-worker world had once hinted at to me. I was walking and working and living in the 3D world and I had lost my connection to my soul and the universal consciousness. I had forgotten the energy and the vibration of the 5D world that I had known as a child and I had lost my 'I am'; my divinity.

Thankfully, Spirit would not let that happen. My guides refused to watch me vibrate lower than the frequency they know I should reside, certainly not since I had worked so hard to connect with like-minded souls. I had tasted that connection again through Reiki and knew that it existed, and they knew I knew. And one day, I finally heard my inner voice again. The one that refused to give up on me – the one that reminded me that I was a *Queen Bee* and that like the Queen Bee, I needed to protect myself and remind myself of my importance and place in the world. So, I left. I took my children and I left. I knew that in doing so, I would lose everything – my home, my businesses, my partner, my step-child, my sanity - but I did it anyway, and in that moment, I finally broke. The trauma of my life caught up with me and I broke.

So, three years ago, I was perched on a milk crate as a chair and using a foldable camping table as a dining room table all set up within the outside carport. in the middle of winter. I lived there as it was the only place I could afford after losing everything. My kids and I ate outside as the unit was too small to fit a dining table in it (even a small one) and so instead, I set up the makeshift dining room every day outside. I was a single Mum, since leaving, and my kids (then 5 & 3 years old respectively) saw only an adventure and fun with Mum. They did not see the tears in my eyes, as I felt shame for what I could not provide for them. They did not see the fear that was lightly veiled behind my eyes as I struggled to work out how I could keep this meagre roof over their heads and they did not see the deep, deep despair and grief that lay on and around my heart at the loss and betrayal and heartache I was enduring.

As I adapted into this experience, the trauma of when I was 10, 14 & 16 came crashing down on me. My parent's divorce and my mother's ill health weighed heavily on my mind and the recent betrayal of my safety and security through violence from the person that I thought loved me, plagued me. The isolation and the loneliness engulfed me. The searching and the trauma consumed and threatened me, and I hit rock bottom. I checked out - out of this painful, emotive filled world. Out of the world that I had not really fit in anyway and that I had always struggled to find myself within. And I attempted to take my own life.

After I did, I lay on the floor of my bedroom where my five-year-old daughter later found me and called for help, and I cried and cried inside. I cried for the empathic girl that never truly understood the world around her. I cried for the universe and the pain (and beauty) that it possessed. I cried for the soul that I was, that was unable to understand the depth of the emotion that I continually felt and how to sanction it and live with it. And as I cried, the most miraculous thing happened. My daughter ran to her room and grabbed from her bedside table, a Rose Quartz crystal and placed it in my hand.

As she did, she bent down to my ear and whispered to me, "It's okay Mum, because this crystal is love. It will love you".

I woke later that day with the crystal still in my hand and a new understanding of the world that I had taken nearly thirty-five years to understand. Life is love! All we do is love. Unconditional love of the Earth, of the Universe and of each other.

Over the course of the next few months, I found myself stripped bare, but I did not care. My kids were forced from their private school they attended due to my finances being cut off and both of my businesses were placed into administration. But, despite losing everything, I started to smile again. I had lost everything, I was homeless and drowning in crippling debt, but I knew that it would all be okay. I knew then that the world is not the material things I had lost. Those emotions I felt were a gift to a greater understanding of the world around me and not a curse to be burdened with. Instead, when we embrace Spirit and the Universe and allow the flow of energy to come and go, then we can access the consciousness of the universe itself and be part of, and one, with it.

Today, I am whole and healed. Today I walk and exist within the 5D world once more and I have everything that I want in life and continue to attract even more to me daily. Today, I walk and work within a world of the light workers, as a spiritual teacher to others. Today, I am an energy healer and use and channel Reiki and Crystal energy to assist others in their own awakenings. I am a believer in the power of positive thought and the Law of Attraction and Manifestation. Today, I am one with the collective consciousness and I understand that energy is **love**. I understand that where our mind goes, energy flows and I understand that we are all connected, because I can feel it all. I always have!

Hitting rock bottom gave me a wondrous opportunity to **stop**. To stand still for just a moment in time and re-evaluate everything that I knew to be true. To look inside myself, deep(!) inside myself and remind myself who I am and that I was loved. I was able to be still and be with my mind (even as broken as my mind was) and form a new vision of what I wanted in my life and what that life looked like. I was able to see the world objectively and from a deeper understanding of how I was (and always had been) connected to it. Today, I am connected to myself and my highest truth and I am walking a path of enlightenment – I AM AWAKE!

The universe's signs and apparitions, to me, are (and always were) messages. They are the signs and the stories of a life lived and filled with lessons and trauma, ones of healing and hope and definitely of connection and understanding. So, if you too see spirits, or if your child (as mine has) tells you that there are always people behind him and he is scared, if your daughter says her angels visit her in her sleep, or you just see that 'something' out of the corner of your eye and know it was actually a 'someone' - then I challenge you to listen closer, to feel more deeply, to sit in stillness and connect to hear the message they bring you. As sometimes, the messages of comfort and support may be exactly what you need to get through what is coming or will allow you to open your eyes and prepare yourself and be ready for the wonderful and amazing things the universe is bringing to you.

My journey as an empath has not been an easy one and it is not filled with wondrous stories of happiness. Instead, it has been one of survival, hope and healing. Being an adult empath is much easier than when I was a child, as I have a greater understanding now of what clairsentience is. But, more importantly, I am now connected with my inner self and my higher self and now, when I feel an emotion, I can 'let it go'. I can literally say in my head "okay, thank you, I release that now", and the emotion I was just feeling – rage, sorrow, hurt, anger, love, fear – will pass and leave me again with my own feelings connected to myself. And, as an energy healer, that is so, so important.

So, how did I achieve this? How did I make this happen? I asked the universe for it! I told the universe I wanted it. I wrote it down. I created vision boards. I meditated, I learned Reiki, so I could connect with Universal life force energy for self-healing. I connected with the crystal kingdom and used their medicine to manifest even more into my life. I sat in a space of stillness and found myself, and I told that girl (my inner child) to show me the path of happiness, and I walk that path each and every day since.

I believed in myself. I trusted myself and I fought *damn hard* every step of the way to be here today, sharing this story with you all.

I did learn one very important thing throughout this journey, though. Time is eternal and when we connect with our own being that exists in the eternal realms, then we no longer fret for tomorrow, or next week, or last year or yesterday. Instead, we focus on now. Here. This instant - and we live!

Remember – where you are, is not who you are.

So, if you are reading this and nodding your head and going, yes, yes that's me… then know this. As an empath we feel both the positive *and* the negative. We feel deeply (in the core of our being and the centre of our hearts), and we, just like anyone else, need to acknowledge and release that emotion when it is felt, in order to not take it on energetically and remain balanced. Accept the emotion is being felt. Acknowledge it and then release it as you need. Because I used to think there was something wrong with, but now I realise – no, I am perfect. I am just an empath!

Belinda

The Sensitive Empath

Christin Ewald

You picked it up from a stranger on the street", said my Reiki Practitioner. I reached out to her because I'd had nightmares for quite some time. It was unusual for me. I'd dreamt of a couple of men breaking into my house, coming into my bedroom at night in the dark and dragging me off the bed. I tried hard to stop myself from imagining any further things. I tried to think of something positive, but the fears and visions came back, frightening me. "A stranger?" I asked, "I picked it up from a stranger?" "Yes, you are very sensitive." Wow. I had no idea what it really meant back then. I was sensitive? I picked up someone else's fear? Are people walking down the street afraid of getting raped? How does this even work? And what is an empath?

Today, being an empath to me means that we are

very sensitive; particularly sensitive to our emotions and our environment. I feel like I am very sensitive to the food I eat, to the people I surround myself with, and activities that I do. I pick up on other people's emotions. I feel more than just me. I can tune into people and feel what's going on for them. I can sometimes also feel people talk about me. I find people talking to me about things that they have been carrying for ages.; something they had suppressed for so long or/and weren't able to talk to anyone else about. The coolest thing of all is, I can hear my own inner guidance clearer and better. I also feel like I have a very gentle heart that wants to love everyone. Of course, this is fantastic, but I learned that I have to love myself first. The most important lesson for me of all time has been: *love myself as priority.* The love I wish someone else would give me (e.g. a partner, the care of a mother or the protection of a father) is what I learned and still am learning to give to myself.

Setting strong, firm boundaries is very important as well. Through setting boundaries and loving myself, I take back my power and am responsible for the energy I bring to the world, and free myself from needing any outside influences to make me feel loved, cared for, or anything else I wish to feel or experience. There is no more waiting for someone to love and fulfill me. I am very proud of having established a behaviour like this. I found and created a lot of other tools as well. Many are very child friendly because they are playful and easy to apply and understand. I use them with my 3-year-old child and he loves them. Before I share them with you, I would like to remind you that you are not alone.

As an empath, we attract many challenges. We can find ourselves being bullied, getting into addictions and attracting abusive relationships. My greatest challenge is the emotional side of it. I feel a *lot*, including other's energies. I started smoking at fourteen years old, which is the age our emotional body develops. I never learned to deal with my emotions and needs in a healthy way. I quit smoking when I was twenty-five, learning that I had smoked cigarettes instead of giving myself what I actually needed: food, rest, celebration, exercise, validation, and so forth. I would smoke every time I was tired or hungry, or to reward myself or to relax. It is a completely new life without smoking. I taste more, I feel better - lighter, happier, freer. I smell better. I feel happier. You know when someone asks you, "are you a smoker?" I was always very aware of how guilty and ashamed I felt when I said yes. I feel so happy now when people ask me, and I say, "No. I quit."

Another great challenge I've had over the years are relationships. I tend to attract unhealthy and abusive relationships. Now, how to deal with them? Love yourself. This might become a theme throughout this writing, and you'll notice I say it a lot, but it worked a great deal for me.

Love yourself as a priority.

To me, attracting abusive relationships is very much like being love addicted. You are trying to fill an empty feeling with a person. That is very unhealthy because you give the power to meet your own needs away, and hand it to someone else. I have done this. I've handed my power over to someone else until I felt so stretched out, I wasn't even aware I was stretched out. I couldn't distinguish at that point anymore what was mine and what was someone else's. Hence, why I felt confused where the nightmares came from that I mentioned at the beginning of this story. Now, how did I get out of this? How did I pull myself together? And how do you protect yourself from attracting unhealthy relationships?

Tools. I started doing little meditations. I checked in with myself and my chakras. I learned to clear my energy and protect it. I would imagine myself being wrapped up in a bubble of colour of my choice and imagined it surrounding myself. I read Rachel Scoltock's book, "Loving your Sensitive Self". She gives great tools to play with to protect and clear your energy throughout the day. I highly recommend reading it. It led me to more tools and helped me get strong on my journey and pull my energies back to myself, as well as taking responsibility for myself and my own energy.

I started talking to God. The Creator, Universe, All. Whatever you want to call it. I call it God. I was contemplating whether to mention this as point number 1, but it was number 2 on my journey. A very powerful thing. I think I needed it in that order because I didn't believe. I didn't believe in a higher power or a god, or anything like that. I was raised very open minded. Coming across God was really not planned, although I had come across him before. I prayed intuitively as a child. How attuned I was.

Later, I did start to talk to God, when I found myself at my lowest, darkest point. I read in Steven K. Scott's book, "The Richest Man Who Ever Lived". That God wants to hear all of your problems. He wants to know everything. He wants to be your best friend. He wants you to just read it yourself. So, on that night, when I was lying in bed, crying my eyes out from being in so much pain once again, I thought about what I read. I looked into the air. I laughed. I said, "Dear God", and carried on. For the first time ever, I was honest and 100% open. I was truthful with how I felt and what was going on. I didn't know the outcome of my prayer. All I said was, 'God'. I explained honestly how I felt about everything. I continued, and I read this prayer in a book as well:

"If anything has to leave my life, then please let that happen with ease and grace. This, or something better please. Thank you. Amen. And, so it is."

And, the course of action took place. I talk and pray often. It works. Soon, I came across more tools and teachings. I learnt to love myself in new ways and followed my guidance more and more.

Step up and out, and always be true to yourself. That is difficult at times, because we get scared or worried, or don't see a path, but please be advised that there is always a way. Sometimes, it can just be challenging to figure out *how* to deal with it. Especially in abusive situations or addictions, we are not always aware of how to help ourselves, because other people's behaviour can be beyond our perceptions. So, please seek help if you need to. Yell out. Cry out. Anything.

Even if you don't know what's wrong, say it as it is: "I don't know what's wrong". That is all it takes sometimes. There is *always* someone who hears you.

God is the first for sure, and He sends help in ways that you cannot imagine. He is everywhere and always available for you. I pray that this writing reaches you. If not in physical form, then in the knowing and energy of it. Please know that you can always ask for guidance and help. Reach out. It might feel new and random, or weird for you to pray, but God is always there; always hearing you. It is up to you to ask and listen.

I didn't grow up this way. Today, I wish I would have. It might have made my life much easier in many ways. But hey, we are all learning, right? And, I am happy to show you that you are never too old to learn to live this way, or to learn new ways, or to start over again, or to tune in! It is never too late. Nothing out there in the world is too embarrassing or too *anything* for you not to share. Someone has always been through it, trust me! There is always someone that can relate in some way. It is often our own perception of things that makes us believe we will not be able to get through this or survive that. Please know that you can handle and go through anything. *Anything*. Even those moments where you tell yourself, "I can't". Trust me; you *can*. I did. And, if I can do it, you can do it too. There is nothing special about me. I am human. You are human. We are the same, but different, and that is okay. You are always loved and looked after.

Allow yourself to think positive and you will see that

there is always a way, and it is not as troublesome as it may look. If it is, please reach out. You are loved. And, even if you lose everything, there is still so much to live for. *So much.* The world is so much bigger than we think or perceive it is. Life always goes on. Breathe. All is well. It might not seem that way right now, but it is. I can't convince you it is. I can't make you see. You've got to open your eyes yourself.

I used to hate life. I used to find it unfair, cruel and shockingly dark. That is such a small part of this planet. There is so much love out there for all of us. So much that it often makes me cry tears of joy. Just these birds outside of my window enjoying the rain, playing in the tree. It is beautiful. What do you find beautiful? What do you love? Where do you see yourself in five or ten years?

I love you so much. Do you love yourself? I really hope this story helps you on your journey.

Loving myself. The biggest milestone in my history of learning so far, is that I learned to love myself. Instead of expecting my partner to love me and give me all that I needed, I started to give it to myself. I started to treat myself better. I went to therapy to seek help and saw nurses to get help with my child. I cooked myself tea, took breaks, set healthy boundaries and worked on myself. Really, it was not the relationship after all that was the problem. It had been me all along.

I remember the moment my son was born. I was looking for a way to keep him as pure and loving as he was in that moment. So, I embarked on a self-development journey. All of that led me to understand that we are so much more than our challenges. Our challenges truly are a gift for us to grow and learn more about ourselves and love. I truly believe that, and I truly see now, how important it is to get my message out there and provide even more information, tools and education for you to make it easy to find your way to the light.

Being an empath can be a challenging journey, but it can also be a lot of fun, and once you get the swing of it, you will enjoy it. I am thirty years old and I am learning every day. I fail, I make mistakes, I fall, I learn, I get back up, I rest. Allow yourself to be vulnerable. Be honest with yourself. That is so important. And, if you feel comfortable with it, hand it all over to God. Ask the angels and your spiritual support team for help and guidance. Thank them for their help; they are loving it.

Now, last, but not least of all, I want to share with you my all-time favourite meditation with the unicorns to protect and clear myself.

Sit down quietly somewhere or lie down if you can. Breathe in deeply, into your belly. Breathe out. Breathe in again and breathe out slowly. Do it again.

Imagine white light coming from the top of your head all the way into your being. It travels down from your head into your forehead, ears, face, filling up your body. The light is travelling down into your chest, your arms, your hands. You are breathing deeply, in and out. Imagine the light further filling your belly, hips, legs, all the way down to your feet, into the earth. All of this is grounding you.

Now, imagine rainbow colours surrounding you - protecting you from all negative energies. Imagine the unicorns coming in, supporting you. Call upon them. Ask them for their help. Do it until you feel a unicorn horn coming out of your forehead. Imagine yourself coming back into your body and wiggle your fingers and toes.

When I count to three, you will be in the present moment, remembering everything that happened. You feel grounded and safe. One, two, three.

Before I wrap it up, I want to mention that during the process of writing this, I realised that I do feel empathy for the people I attracted back then. I have no idea what it must feel like to be in their shoes and I do have to own my part in the story as well, and all the behaviour that caused the situation. That is all. Focus on you and your actions. Everything else is outside of your control. Although, you do gain more control over everything once you learn to control yourself. It is amazing! Never act out of pity or because you feel bad for someone.

What is your favourite tool? What do you get out of it all? How would you like to respond to what is happening to you? With gratitude, always. Writing for me is very healing. I could do that all day. I have learned so much sharing this.

Thank you,

Being an Empath

Danielle Renee – Holistic Therapist, Writer

The word empathy means experiencing emotions that match another person's emotions. It is the ability to feel and share another's emotions. Having empathy is understanding how another is feeling and being able to see all the contributing factors to their current emotional state.

To me, an empath is an individual who does have empathy and identifies another individual's emotions. An empath has a deep understanding of how others are feeling, however, the difference between having empathy and being an empath is that an empath takes on the emotions they are feeling from others, and feels these emotions deeply, as if they were their own. The emotions are felt so deeply that often the empath experiences them and does not realise that they are not their own.

Being an empath isn't easy. About a year ago, I came to the realisation that I am an empath, and fully understood how this gift has affected me over the course of my life. Through further self-development, I have learnt what this gift means to me, and how it can be helpful in our daily life.

When I was younger and at school, I was affected by other people's actions. Children would do something to someone, just for fun. I didn't understand their actions and words, even though others would laugh and think it was fun. At the time, I thought, 'How could this be fun? You have hurt another person'. I would feel that child's pain and sadness. School wasn't easy, and I was teased at times like most children were. However, when I was teased it would hurt my feelings at a deep level; to the core. I was sensitive then, as I am sensitive now. I would withdraw and chose to play on my own in the playground until whatever was in the air blew over. Some days I would come home sad and would have quiet time to process the day; feeling hurt and not understanding why. As time went on, I went into survival mode. I was sick of being hurt and teased, so I stood up for myself and put on a hard front of, "Don't mess with me!" which was a strategy to protect myself and to buffer some of the teasing and school yard games.

One theme throughout my life is that I was and still am the go to person for other people's problems. I would help someone feel better. I would listen and respond, and a deep wisdom would pour out of me. I would know how that person felt and was able to offer support and strategies to be able to empower that person. Some of the situations that people were experiencing I had never experienced myself, however, there would be something within my words that would resonate with that person. A healing or release of some sort would take place. I would reflect after the conversation, and wonder where the wisdom had come from, and how what I'd said had resonated for that individual. What would come through me wasn't just advice; I had an understanding and empathy for that person. Afterwards, I would feel as though I had made a difference and was able to assist others to heal their pain. These experiences made me feel whole. A part of me felt I had healed something, too.

In my twenties, I was drawn to natural therapies. I began my journey as a healer studying Reiki, Crystals, Bach flower essences and Shiatsu, to name a few. I found these tools valuable in healing my own emotions and releasing what wasn't mine. I used these techniques to heal myself as I often experienced a high level of sickness. If there was a virus going around, I got it. Later, I learnt that the emotions someone was experiencing was coming out in sickness. I would pick up on that emotion and get sick too. I was able to start working on myself to understand all of this better.

Being an extremely sensitive person, I would often feel an emotion deeply, which did affect me physically. A trip to the shops or going out in public was a challenge at times, from picking up on other people's emotions. I would notice I would leave the house happy and come home angry. I would react to situations, and that was so unlike me.

I then realised what was going on around me, wasn't about me – it was about the other person and how they were feeling. I came to understand that all the emotions I was feeling weren't mine. I was so busy being in the emotion, that I didn't even realise this. Once I differentiated between which emotions were mine, and which were not, I was able to get myself back on track. I analysed my feelings and why was I feeling this way.

If I couldn't rationally link the emotion to anything that had happened, I knew that it was someone else's emotion I was carrying.

Most of my life I have suffered some level of anxiety and worry. The last few years I have gone through a lot of anxiety, and during one period, it increased where I was anxious a lot of the time. I just didn't feel well. I was nauseous, I had body aches and pains, and fatigue, to name a few symptoms. Some of this may have been my own emotions I was holding as pain in certain areas. Some of it wasn't mine at all.

About a year ago during an intense period of anxiety, I had a revelation; an epiphany. I couldn't trace where my anxiety was coming from. I was anxious all the time with no known cause. It was then that I came to the realisation that I am an empath. The anxiety I was feeling was someone else's. I knew I was a sensitive person and a healer; I had done so much self-work and healing. But, I realised that my whole life of feeling different, watching what people did to each other and not understanding, was because I was an empath. It was then, that I understood why certain experiences had come into my life. Why I was often told things no one else would be told, and why people instinctively knew that I wouldn't share what they had told me. There was an unwritten code of ethics that I had within me; an unspoken trust. People would trust me and were always thankful for my support. This was all part of being given the gift of being an empath. Knowing what it meant to be empathic helped me to understand why I was drawn to certain things, why people would tell me things, and why I was always a 'go to' person.

I understand others' emotions. I know how they feel, because I experience their emotions within myself.

I can feel another person's pain, their sorrow, heart ache or anger. Some of the emotions I absorb can make me physically sick, and this still happens from time to time. I have to be mindful of what I am experiencing and check within my internal system; questioning if they are my own emotions. If they aren't, I ask for them to be removed.

Empaths will often have other people share their thoughts, feelings or a situation with them, that often wouldn't be shared with anyone else. An empath has this innate ability to offer support, empowerment and have incredible listening skills. An empath is able to tune into their own, and others' *deeper* feelings to assist in healing.

I am a clairvoyant and a healer. Through these gifts and being an empath, I have learnt to manage this gift in healthy ways through various self-help and self-healing techniques. I practice daily exercises of grounding and protection for self-maintenance, and I have shared some of these for you later in this book.

I hope my story sheds light on what it is like to be an empath. Being an empath is not an easy path to travel. I will often feel emotions more deeply than others; however, it has the hidden blessing of being able to be of service to others through our insight, understanding, compassion, and empathy. It provides a wonderful opportunity for continual growth, learning and understanding, that can be passed on to others.

Danielle

Love is my Superpower

Dr. Dawn Karima PhD

Creator,
Nights when the beat of a drum is legion,
When Warriors rise and stomp under the moon,
We Women rise, too.

Open our shawls and promise plenty,
Swear none will go hungry, be lost or unloved.
Days when the sun goes down on Ceremony,
We are there, too,

Moccasins aligning our souls with the sky,
Firmly plant our lives in this Earth.

Tribes last forever, when we honor Spirit first.

D rums thunder in the powwow arena, while tribal dancers swirl in the circle, making a mélange of beads and feathers. My moccasins move in time with the singers' low vocals, as I follow the footsteps of my family. As a two-time Global Music Award Winner, a Native American Music Award Winner and Indigenous Artist Activist Award Winner, I host a syndicated, award-winning radio show, "A Conversation with Dawn Karima". My days are filled with exciting twists and demanding turns that require spiritual, social, emotional and physical wholeness. I desire to infuse my music and media with Love and Light. Finding wholeness in my Indigenous heritage helps me to use my gifts and talents to uplift others.

When I became a woman, I went to ceremony. Elder women taught me that to be a woman is to "carry the people". They gave me a shawl with swinging long fringes, to represent my willingness to feed my family and my community, emotionally and spiritually. Women are good medicine, I learnt. Life givers are the energy of the Earth; the shields of the sky. Some people call those of us with the ability to bear pain for the people and to exchange it for healing, "empaths" and declare that we are part of the "New Age". The Elders shrug. For Tribal People, this gift of spiritual alchemy is as old as the ancestors.

I pray in our stomp dance way. Turtle shell rattles wreath my legs, as each dance step I make carries the prayers of the people. Rocks fill the rattles, making music as ladies dance in a circle along with our men, who sing songs as ancient as the stars.

Balancing my career as a broadcaster, artist, educator and speaker with participation in Indigenous spiritual paths magnifies my Higher Self above my emotional self. Smudging with sage and cedar, dancing to drumbeats, shaking turtle shells in stomp dance, praying, fasting and singing with my tribal community helps to cleanse my soul and create clarity in my mind. Such clarity and peace are vital to my creativity; especially since my heart's desire is to make music and media that educates, enlightens and edifies my audience. People call me an Empath, a Prophetess, an Oracle; but, all I know is that I am making medicine.

Imagine that I decide to show you the Native American Reservation that is my home. We'll hike to see if we can see a bear cub, and we'll stop to see the majestic mountain views. Maybe we'll go into the hills and hollers and find a little church, so we can enjoy some good country singing. Pretend you're following me. I'm leading the way and all of a sudden, you think, "Hey, what does she know? Why am I following her? My car is just as good as hers. I'm just as good a driver as she is, so why am I following her around?" So, you strike out on your own.

How long will it be before you find yourself lost? Yet, getting lost is completely unnecessary, since if you just followed me you would have ended up at a delightful destination. Well, guess what? It's that way spiritually, too.

Sometimes, when we take off on our own and decide to go our own way, we end up needing spiritual help, emotional help, mental help and help from other people. That's what tribal culture is meant to do, to provide us with a guide to bring us back into balance and restore our souls. Our ceremonial songs, dances and prayers provide valuable vibrations that inspire me to write songs, author books, speak motivationally and help others who are enduring difficult circumstances.

Each time I reconnect with my tribal traditions, I remember that Love is my first language. I give Love, I gather Love. I walk in love. Love Creator and love others is my mission and Love is my superpower.

The precious fruit of the Spirit
Secretly brought
In thoughts
From the visions of the night
To the Empaths
Who turn on our beds.

Instead,
Our sleep flees
Until the Spirit answers,
We rise and raise our hearts in prayer,
Shake shells under songs,
Heal the heartsick and raise the spiritually dead.

That said,
We thank Creator, sitting on the circle of the world.
When our light sets the world on fire,
The tree of life and all its vines are ours.

Dawn

Raising the vibration of the planet... one person at a time

Debra Anderton

Albany, Western Australia, is a beautiful part of the world to live in. This region is a spiritual nexus and is home to many beautiful people and practitioners. I have called it home for twenty-four years, after moving here with my infant daughter in 1993. I have spent a lot of time over the years learning about raising my vibration. I have visited psychics, reiki healers, shamans, aura readers, and tarot readers, and it was all because I was curious as to how their gift worked and I wanted to learn about all things spiritual. I have bought and read many books on the subject, seeking knowledge. At the age of forty-four years, I describe myself as a perpetual student!

When my daughter came into my life, I wanted to make our lives as incredible as they could be. Hence, the quest for enlightenment began around the time I became a parent, although in hindsight, I always had an inner knowing and awareness of spirit.

From a very young age, I've found myself helping people through difficult times. I think this is the biggest indicator of Empath behaviour; the need to help. I was in my early twenties when I realised I had empathic tendencies. I've always been a good listener, but I noticed that I'd attract people right when they were feeling very low about a situation and I was able to raise them up, so they could go forth and face it confidently. I've had many people tell me that I helped them through a tough situation. While it is nice having the validation, it is really not necessary. My intention is to always come to a situation from a place of love, and I hope you feel as though my advice is grounding and resourceful.

Empath qualities
Scientists call it energy. Religion calls it spirit. Street folk call it a vibe. To me, it's all the same. We all have a soul and our soul is made from energy. Life around us is made up of energy also, and we feel it resonating. Some people feel this more than others. We are known as Empaths.

For me, being an empath is about being perceptive and picking up on the vibe of any situation. It is about feeling warmth towards, sympathy for, and concern about other people. We also have the tendency to feel discomfort and concern when witnessing others' negative experiences and experience high levels of personal distress. It is about hearing what is being said in a conversation and equally as important, hearing what is *not* being said. As an empath, I can feel energy and spirits in buildings by the sudden drop in temperature. I hear voices, the phone ringing and knocking at the door whenever I'm in the shower. Water is a conduit for spiritual energy. This became really apparent when I was living by myself for the first time. It took me a while to stop getting out of the shower mid-way through, as there was never anyone at the door or on the phone.

Each object has an energy, which has led me to own very few objects and build a house from scratch, so I don't have to feel the history or energy of past tenants. The history of places and objects can feel overwhelming, so learning how to cope with this is vital. Spending long periods of time with other people can be really draining; whether they are your favourite people or colleagues you have no choice but to spend time with. I know when people are in distress and can assist them, usually while everyone around me is totally unaware anything is amiss. Most of all, it's about self-reflection and really having a deep understanding of my place in the world and how I can influence and help others.

I have learnt that it is really important to base all decisions from a place of love, and not fear.

Energy can be changed incrementally, and I believe that if you choose to think positively a little bit at a time, this will increase more and more rapidly. This in turn, will increase the positivity in your life. I'm sure you will still have some dark moments or dark days, but if you improve your life, the dark times should decrease as your energy increases.

There are two different platforms of thought. For example, I choose to work a lot because I value independence and really enjoy financial freedom. Some people would say they work so they don't lose their house and become homeless. We are basically doing the same thing, although one thought process has beneficial energy based in love attached to it, and one has detrimental energy based in fear attached to it. It is my belief that if you live your life from a place of love, you experience more love. If you live your life from a place of fear, you will in turn, experience more fear. This is my interpretation of manifesting situations in your life.

Nature / Animals
Having an affinity with nature and all creatures is a big part of this world. You can always tell a lot about a person by the way they treat animals.

I have recently seen a couple of videos on social media where dogs are visibly crying. They were sobbing their little hearts out and crying real tears. One dog had lost his person and was crying on the grave. Another dog was taken to a shelter and cried when he realised that his people had left him behind. This is enough to bring me to tears for days. It is very hard to get these images out of my mind. Dogs and all other animals have feelings and deserve to live in a world where they have love, affection, shelter, warmth, food, water and above all else, safety. I feel great distress from knowing animals are mistreated and neglected, just the same way that I feel great distress from knowing people - especially children - are mistreated or neglected.

The news and social media are filled with tragedies and even though I am aware that awful things happen in the world, I don't think it is necessary for me to know the details and see graphic images of things that I have no control over. This brings up two key points, namely:

1. Animals - domestic and wild - have a right to live their lives without harm and neglect from mankind.

2. It's a good idea to turn the TV and social media off sometimes so you don't become bombarded with horrific and graphic content, which can scar you for life.

Feeling things so deeply, so emotionally, is sad and unproductive. Some people will see an awful injustice and are compelled to go on a quest to champion a cause and that is absolutely wonderful. One person really can make a difference. What is not great is feeling helpless at the endless cruelty man is capable of, when you aren't in a position to change it.

Examples of my experiences
I find myself having deep and meaningful conversations with strangers on a regular basis. This happens very quickly and I'm not sure if people sense that I'm a great listener, or whether I sense that people need to talk to someone who cares, and I prompt them. Both situations are probably true.

Teenage Party Situation

When I was a teenager, about fifteen years old, I went to a party. I remember talking to a gorgeous and popular guy in a separate part of the house to where the rest of the party was held. I was able to see that Ryan was upset, while everyone else seemed oblivious. We talked for hours and I remember him giving me a hug or two. There was nothing intimate in it. He was just grateful that I was listening and giving him advice, and basically being there for him. Other people kept walking by and commenting that I should leave him alone; he had a girlfriend and I had no business spending time with him. I have no idea why their opinions were that I was doing something wrong and he received no comments at all. All I knew was that he was distressed, and I was in a position to be there for him. I remember leaving the party knowing that I helped someone, and the loss of friends didn't matter to me. If they were really my friends, they wouldn't have been so awful to me.

I knew at a young age that helping people was more important than being popular.

Friend Situation

I went with a group to a friends' house that was just out of town on a small farm near Tunney, WA. I was pregnant at the time, so I must have been nineteen years old. Brad was my age and both of his parents had died and his sister worked in another town, so he lived all alone in the big farmhouse. We played pool and the others had a few drinks. Basically, we were just hanging out with good company. On this night, I remember walking into the living room and the temperature dropped by about 10-15 degrees. No one else noticed, so I asked him if anything had happened in this room and he told me this was where his mum died. No one else in the group could feel the change in temperature. This was the first time this had happened to me and has happened several times since. Now, when I feel the temperature drop suddenly, I know that spirit is close, and I don't need to bring it to anyone else's attention. I just trust that I know.

Aeroplane Situation

I was on an aeroplane journey from Sydney to Perth, Australia two years ago and I found myself sitting next to a gentleman named John, who was only a few years older than I am. I watched a movie for the first part of the journey. After that, John and I started talking. He told me that he lived in Sydney with his wife and young son and that he was on his way to South Africa as his dad had passed away and he was going back to finalise his affairs. He was worried about the financial cost of having to make the journey and the lost hours at work. He went on to say that he had left South Africa many years earlier and only went back when he absolutely had to. This would be the last time he would be going there as his mum had passed a few years previous, and he no longer had any relatives there. He was not looking forward to going, and he actually felt really anxious about it all.

It didn't surprise me at all that we were having this deep conversation within minutes of talking to each other, as this is commonplace for me. I asked him if he wanted to know what I thought about his situation (I don't assume everyone wants my opinion, so it doesn't hurt to ask first). He said he was interested in what I thought. I went on to tell him that firstly, his parents both lived to a decent age, which is a wonderful thing. Secondly, he didn't need to do this alone. His mum had passed some years previously, so she would have healed on the other side and been strong enough to call on for help. I told him to talk to her in the house while he was there, while he was packing up the belongings or selling them, before he was to liaise with the lawyer, or whatever he was doing. I told him she would be delighted to have him home again, and proud that he was able to make the journey and finalise everything. He could then return to his family in Sydney after closing the chapter that was South Africa (with many unpleasant memories).

John said my words gave him comfort and going back wouldn't be as bad as he had first thought. He was thrilled at the thought of his parents being alive and well on the other side of the veil. I guess while he was focusing on the negative side of the situation, I was able to remind him of the positive side. Most situations have good and bad points about them. Balance is the key. He thanked me and said our chat had helped him immensely.

FIFO Situation
FIFO (Fly In, Fly Out work) is an industry rife with mental illness. People spend incredibly long amounts of time away from their loved ones. They miss events and special occasions, and even just the day-to-day life with their kids that they are missing out on hurts deeply. Suicide is common. Recently, at one of the mine sites I was situated at, I was working on the front counter and a man came in about a maintenance issue in his room. He lodged the

maintenance request and I felt that he wasn't okay, so I asked him the question "Are you okay?" He asked if I had any phone numbers to call if he wanted to talk to someone. I told him that we certainly did. We have a list of EAP (Employee Assistance Program) numbers, which lists contact numbers for each contractor working on the site, as well as general phone numbers such as LifeLine and Beyond Blue etc. I had a look for the list on our pinup boards in the reception area but couldn't find it. I told him that I had recently seen it in the common area, which was close by and asked him to walk with me while I looked for it. He seemed pleased by my company and came with me while I looked in the obvious places. I still couldn't find it. I told him that there was a psychologist in the medical centre next door and that he was more than welcome to go and talk to someone in person, while I went back to the office and printed off a copy of the list for him. He asked if I really thought going to the medic's office was a good idea, and I told him that it was absolutely no trouble and the service is there for situations like these. I went to the office and printed another copy of the list and took it to the medics' office where he was in the waiting room. He thanked me, and I told him I was glad I could help. This interaction would have taken fifteen minutes at the most.

The following day, he came into my work and asked if he could talk to me privately. I went around to his side of the counter and he thanked me for taking the time to help him the day before. He said I was very kind; right when he needed it most. I didn't make him feel like a nuisance at all. He said he was planning on taking his own life and that after talking to me, he felt better. The psychologist also helped him and gave him advice. He gave me the biggest, warmest hug and smiled at me. By sensing that he was not okay, spending the time to help him find the information he needed, guiding him to the psychologist and basically speaking to him in a kind manner, I made a difference to one man in his time of need.

Strategies you can use

It's fundamental that empaths and sensitive people recognise others who resonate on a lower vibration. I call them 'energy vampires' (people who drain your energy) and have clear strategies to deal with this. I've collated a few ideas for resonating at a higher frequency and how to deal with people who deplete your energy. Please read on.

Be your own Best Friend

First and foremost, each person must be his or her own best friend. Just imagine if your best friend in the whole world came to you with a situation. How would you speak to them? You would be kind, a great listener, supportive and helpful. Do this for yourself, also. Be kind to yourself, let your internal voice be soothing and learn as much as you can. Knowledge is strength. Invest in yourself. Study, read, learn from other people and find a mentor. Continuously learn and grow throughout your life. Keep busy. Surround yourself with kind people. Your self-worth will increase. Your self-respect will increase. Your confidence will increase. Ultimately, your happiness will increase. This is the goal.

It is perfectly okay to recognise that we have negative emotions sometimes. Every one of us has a bad day sometimes or a significant event that we wish had not occurred. We are human. We are souls having a human experience and life isn't always wonderful. Acceptance of this is crucial. It is a part of life to feel sadness, anger, betrayal, jealousy, apathy, hate, grief, hurt and other emotions like these. There is absolutely nothing wrong with any one of these emotions; just don't unpack and live there.

Trust your intuition
We all have intuition or gut instinct - whatever you like to call it - and most of us listen and trust it. As an Empath, your intuition is heightened, and you can use this every day to benefit your life and those around you. When you learn to quiet your mind and listen, you can sense good things and bad. Trust it and learn to act on it. You will find more good things happen and less bad things, as you can learn to trust and avoid certain situations.

Volunteering
Volunteer work is a way of giving back to your community, being a good role model and realising that the world is bigger than your circle of friends and family. It is also something you can do to take the focus off your own life for a short time. The shift in focus can be invaluable. You come back to your own situation with fresh eyes. You can also gain new skills, expand your knowledge and meet like-minded people, who may potentially be friends for life. Volunteering also has the added benefit of making you feel good about yourself, which is a part of raising your own vibration.

My daughter (Troi) and I volunteered our time, one day per week for six months at a native Australian animal park in Albany before it opened to the public. We cleaned out animal enclosures and fed and watered the animals. We also brought eucalyptus branches into the koala enclosure, so they had fresh leaves to eat. It was hard work, but so rewarding. Troi loves animals and wanted to work with them when she grew up. I wanted to show her that she could create the life she wanted, gain skills and knowledge, give back to the community and basically steer her life in the direction she wanted to go, all by donating her time once in a while. Her favourite animals at the park were the spotted quolls. I loved the koalas, especially a male named Boof. He would always make his way over to me when I was in the enclosure. Most animals kept their distance, but Boof was really friendly.

Grounding
As an Empath, you will be dealing with energy and emotion a lot. This can leave you feeling depleted or disconnected from reality. I sometimes find I get light headed and to stay grounded, I use the power of Mother Nature. Soaking up the sun's rays is not only regenerative, but a simple pleasure. Walk barefoot either around the house or outside - literally on the earth. The beach is also wonderful and soul cleansing. I personally like to walk along the beach, in the water up to my knees. Sitting near the beach and hearing the waves softly crashing against the shore with seagulls and pelicans flying overhead is a peaceful way to ground yourself and remember that we are small in the big scheme of things. Spending time at a park with lovely trees, flowers and birds can

be really refreshing, also. 'Forest Bathing' therapy is big in Japan at the moment.

Walking among the trees has been scientifically proven to lower your stress levels. Synchronizing your rhythm to the rhythm of nature improves your health and mood.

Spending time with any animal is also grounding. Let your excited dog slobber all over your hands and clothes and thank him for the experience.

I love the feel of a slight breeze on my face. I once had a psychic say to me that I need to live on a hill and have the wind in my face. She said I could breathe easier this way. She also conveyed her confusion by saying that everyone else could breathe without the wind, why couldn't I? I responded by telling her that the breeze enables me to be in the eternal now moment where I focus on it and cease overthinking. I just exist peacefully for a moment in time.

Eating and drinking is a way to ground you quickly. This reminds you that you have a physical body and you are currently existing on the physical plane.

Crystals are from the earth, so naturally I believe that they have grounding qualities. Each type has unique qualities and representations and can be used in a multitude of ways. I have placed crystals and other talismans within the walls of the house that I have recently built. They will never be seen unless someone chooses to renovate. The builder was quite surprised and mocked me a little but ensured that as a paying customer, my request would be granted. By the end of the house build, he had witnessed a few unexplained situations and genuinely asked me whether the crystals helped with the project by keeping it injury, drama and problem free. I told him that I believed the crystals raised the vibration of my property and had protective qualities. He told me he was a believer after spending a year working with me.

Stargazing is a wonderful way to ground yourself. It is calming and serene to be in the moment; looking up at the sky with the Milky Way, dozens of constellations and to see the moon and planets just cruising past. This is magical for everyone, not just Empaths.

If you can't get back to nature, then the next best thing is an app on your phone or electronic device that plays nature sounds. When I have difficulty falling asleep, my favourite is the sound of birds tweeting in a forest with the sound of wind through the trees. The choice is endless, though, so check it out!

Challenge what you hear
I've heard people say that we must only think positive thoughts and if you don't, then bad things will happen, and you only have yourself to blame, as you created the situation with your thoughts. Manifesting what happens in your life is possible, but I believe this view of never thinking a bad thought to be unnatural and warped. I had a friend say to me after reading a book about manifesting wealth, that she isn't a good person. She said she obviously doesn't think enough positive things or say enough

positive things to people. I asked her why she would think this, and she said that she plays lotto and has never won; therefore, she mustn't be a good enough person. Either she has misinterpreted the information, or the book is encouraging unrealistic expectations.

I challenge most of what I hear, and this was definitely one of those times. Firstly, I aim to be kind – always. This is just who I choose to be. Not to make me feel good or to win credit points with other people, but just because I can. If you are being kind to gain something, then this is not kindness, it's business. Being nice to people in order to raise your 'positive points' and win lotto is not kindness. You are only doing it to benefit yourself. Secondly, winning lotto does not mean you are a good person. One has nothing to do with the other. The same way that bad behaviour and negative thoughts do not automatically mean something bad will happen to you. If this were the case, we wouldn't need the judicial system. People would think a bad thought or create a bad deed and they would be instantly struck down by lightning if this philosophy were true.

The way to create a phenomenal future is to educate yourself and behave your way to success. Thinking positively is crucial. Once you think you can do something, then you act on this thought and you are on your way to achieving the goal. Thought plus action equals results.

On another occasion, I mentioned to another friend that after a long and tiring swing in FIFO that I was planning on flying to Perth and sleeping for a while before driving to Albany (a 4.5-hour drive) because I didn't want to just fly to Perth, drive home tired and crash my car into a tree. She was horrified and said that by voicing this aloud, I was manifesting it and making it happen. I challenge this! By flying to Perth and finding somewhere to sleep, I was being sensible and mitigating a potential life-threatening situation. I followed through with my sensible plan and made it home safely. At no time was I in danger simply by stating an undesirable outcome. If it were my time to die, then I believe I would be dead. Talking about dying doesn't make it so.

As a footnote about this 'challenge' idea, it is also a great idea to challenge what you see. For instance, on Facebook I quite often see pictures of a person that someone has posted with a caption that the pictured person has committed some heinous crime. They ask you to share it, so everyone can see this villain. Stop and ask yourself the following questions. *Is it true? Do you know the person? Were you there when they committed this crime? Are you the judge, jury and executioner?* If the answer to any of these questions is no, then keep scrolling and let it pass you by. You do not need to involve yourself in someone else's drama. As an empath, you probably feel obliged to help. Let me make it clear. You most definitely do not need to engage in unnecessary behaviour that is hatred based and has nothing to do with you.

Once you distance yourself from low level drama and attention seeking people, you will find your life is more peaceful and it will start to look like you've always wanted it to look... serene.

Find your tribe

If you can find people who have similar beliefs as you do, then treasure them. Try to build your network by measuring values and beliefs, and by finding people who resonate on a similar frequency to you. Just because you are related to someone biologically, does not mean that person deserves a place in your life. You can select who you spend your time with, guilt free. It is your life and you want to surround yourself and your immediate family with people who are kind and decent, and those that would never cause you harm. Please be especially selective when choosing a life partner. This person will influence your day-to-day life for a very long time (hopefully), so please choose someone who adds value to your life, who will support you during difficult times and who you can do the same for.

Take Control

It's okay to take control of any situation and either give your time to the person seeking your assistance, reschedule a time that suits you, or simply say no. Whether you get paid (as a consultant) or not, it is important for empaths to recognise that life is like a business. You can decide to give someone a little bit of your time, a lot of your time, or none at all. The choice should always be yours. It's also a great idea to be selective with how you spend your time, with whom you spend it and what you spend it on.

You have the power to create a new reality, one day at a time. Please do it consciously.

Plan your day out and once you have an idea of what your day will look like, it is very easy to disregard anything that doesn't fit with that plan. Politely decline any offer that you do not wish to engage in. It is very easy to say, "I have other things on my agenda today, but it was great seeing you!" You need to neither apologise nor make excuses to people. It just is what it is.

Redirect People
You can redirect someone who needs help to another source. There are many people and services available to help people in need. If you make yourself aware of all avenues before you find yourself in a situation, then you will have the information required when you find yourself being drawn into someone's issues. This can be someone in their own life that they can turn to, a professional such as a doctor (general practitioner) or a psychologist. It could also be a practitioner of alternative therapies, such as a clairvoyant, reiki healer, tarot reader, aura reader etc. This is a perfectly legitimate way to assist someone. You don't have to take on everyone's responsibilities personally.

Building positive relationships
Once you have healthy relationships, it is easy to decline anything else. We teach people how to treat us, so ensure you maintain standards and boundaries and everyone will know where they stand. If you are the person (like I was when I was younger) who is always available for a coffee and a chat, you basically give a lot of your precious time and energy away. As soon as I started being selective with whom I gave my time and effort to, my life improved in leaps and bounds. I found that when I said no to people, I had more time to study, gain skills, change career path

and ultimately, I had a lot more time to spend one on one with my daughter. I can't believe it took me a few years to see that I was holding myself back by being too nice and too available. A good friend will understand that you need time to build your own life. Anyone who makes you feel bad is not worth your effort.

Guidance
Guidance is a great option. Teaching people how to help themselves is far reaching and has a ripple effect, whereby others can be taught and helped also. I found this raising my daughter. I quite often heard her talking to her friends when they were teenagers, and she would repeat what I had said to her. In other words, she learnt how to handle situations from me, and passed on the knowledge. Proud parent moment! She has since grown up to be a wonderful young lady who is also sensitive. I think it is both genetically passed on, as well as environmentally.

Self-protection
Self-protection is another strategy. Meditation, visualisation techniques, and white lighting yourself before leaving the house or entering a tumultuous situation, can really help.

It is important to pre-empt problems and protect yourself from the harshness of the world. You can do this by white lighting yourself. This is a visualisation technique where you visualise yourself being surrounded by a white light filled with loving energy. Imagine it circling around your body and shielding you from outside influences. Bring yourself in to the eternal now moment and just breathe. Be aware of where you are, what you can see and hear, and be at peace with the world as it is right now. Everything is fine in this moment. By practicing this technique on a regular basis, you will change the energy frequency of your existence.

Being calm in a tumultuous world is a positive attribute to have. Don't fall into the trap of thinking that you can be calm when the storm passes. The goal is to be calm *during* the storm. If you can learn to be composed in every situation, then you can gain control over yourself and your life. You should be able to deal with any incident that arises in a serene and peaceful manner, no matter how distressing. Any other response is counterproductive. This can take time to master, but it is a lifesaving skill to have and keeps people around you calm during an incident.

Another item that can be beneficial is to learn not to react at all. Not every situation warrants your reaction. If someone is being aggressive or confrontational, it is much better to extract yourself from the situation, than to engage and possibly make the situation worse. My philosophy is to never engage in battle, but if I do, I will never lose. This means that I avoid anger and aggression as much as possible, but if I were to engage in a situation (i.e. to protect a child / animal or for self defence) I would be fierce and a force to be reckoned with.

The moral of this story is to pick your battles. Avoid most of them, but if you must stand up for something, do it with all of your might. Do it intelligently and with gusto. If you find yourself in an argument and the other person is not listening, you need to improve your content, not raise your voice. The bravest / strongest warrior can control him / herself and stay neutral but fight swift and true when necessary. Whether this is physical combat or an intellectual argument of the minds, it has the same basis... self-control.

Safe Haven
Lastly, it is important to have a home where you are free of other peoples' burdens. You need a sanctuary where you can re-energise and heal. I am fortunate to have built a home from scratch on land that has never been lived on before, and I have placed crystals within the walls of my house. There is no residual energy from previous occupants, as there weren't any. This land was a section of a farm. Everyone who visits, mentions how light and fresh the house is, and how uplifting the energy is. It is my safe haven.

If you don't live alone, then create a safe space; perhaps your bedroom or a corner of your living room where you have your comfy chair, throw rug and can enjoy a cup of coffee in peace. It just needs to be a place that you can relax and unwind.

In summary
So, in a nutshell, being an Empath is a blessing and a curse. You feel obligated to help people all the time and need to learn to manage this, so you can stay on track with your own life, and not go off on a tangent too often with somebody else's issues. The blessing part is incredible. I feel as though I have more information to process situations than the average

person, which gives me an advantage. Intuition is a gift. Hone it and use it wisely.

Blessed be.

Deb

Finding your Light

Frannie Lawrence

"Confront the dark parts of yourself, and work to banish them with illumination and forgiveness. Your willingness to wrestle your demons will cause your angels to sing."
August Wilson

(Portland, Oregon; August 2017)

Dear Ellis,

Okay, I'll try to write what I can before we hit the road.

What you're saying is making sense, so much sense, Ellis. I get it, I really do. We have so much in common - I've been where you are. I've experienced portions of my life where I had just accepted that I would continue to live, even though I would most likely never be happy again, but that things would certainly change, eventually, and my only choice was to just hold on. Just hold on, despite the fact that it feels almost entirely hopeless. I didn't even know why I was holding on - what was the point? But, I knew I just had to hold on.

Perhaps this is some innate sense we have to save us from our darkest moments, us empaths who are experiencing being absolutely broken by the world? Perhaps we share this sense that, even though it seems impossible to find, there must be a point to it all. Perhaps, even at the bottoms of the pits of our despair, that hope is the slightest ray of light that's able to make it out of our true selves to our current reality.

Your light is in there, Ellis. Remember what I said about how our programming - everything we learn from the humans around us while our brains are developing - is what creates the cognitive dissonance between who we really are, the shining brightness of our divine souls, and who we are told we need to be? Every bit of programming that contradicts our true nature is another shovelful of debris, collecting around our core, hiding our true selves from our own vision.

When will your light shine? When will it awaken? Do you not feel it being awakened now? This pain is a good sign. It is horrible, and unfair, and you should never have been asked to bear it. And yet you do, and with grace, and compassion for others. Your beauty is in your brokenness, Ellis. You are such a gentle and sweet human, obviously because you have been the victim of rough and unkind humans. You cannot imagine anyone feeling like you have, like you do, so you spread your love and your beauty, creating a world better than the one you find yourself in.

And that's not something that goes away, friend. Of course, the healing power that you spread so freely through the world persists, radiates out from you, continues rolling through the Universe. In a world constantly in search of balance, any light you spread means that much less darkness to be fought. Even if some things may return to the way they once were, or even if you can't save someone, or fix them or their problems, that doesn't mean that your efforts have been pointless. It's impossible for any of us to be happy all of the time, just like it's impossible for anything to persist forever, but it is entirely possible to be truly happy in a moment - and that's what matters. When you bring happiness to others, you change the world forever. I promise. You've changed me forever.

I can't imagine, at this point, having never met such a pure and beautiful soul. And, your purity and your beauty are so special because of your honesty and your vulnerability about the parts of yourself that torment you, and the parts of your experience that have been too ugly to bear.

Perhaps this is part of your purpose? Sharing so freely and honestly and compassionately? Giving others the space to be just as free and honest and compassionate. Leading by example. You're already doing that.

Okay, at this point I'd rather start driving to you, than keep writing to you; I just wanted to get some of those thoughts down.

I'll see you soon.

With love,
Frannie

*** *** ***

(Costa Rica, February 2015)

It's my turn to speak and there's no way I'm going to be able to. Everyone in this quiet circle, in this quiet forest in Costa Rica, who has been quietly ignoring my obvious distress is now looking at me, wondering what it is I'll do next, and what it could possibly be that has me so upset.

I look around, unable to see a thing through my tears, and somehow convey that they should just skip me. The person to my right seizes the opportunity to save me from this mess and begins stating their intention for the coming Ayahuasca ceremony that evening.

I burn from shame. It eats me up that I can't even hold it together long enough to be able to say why I'm sitting here, in this very uncomfortable circle, waiting very uncomfortably for what promises to be a very uncomfortable experience. There isn't even that much to the explanation - I'm sitting here because I want to be less sad. That's it. I just want to not be so impossibly overwhelmed by this sadness.

Everyone else in the circle finishes stating their intentions, and while they do, I pull myself together. Without the pressure of an impending statement of intention, I'm fairly recovered by the time we break to go our separate ways until the ceremony.

Hannah, still a stranger, pulls me aside. She asks me if I'm okay, if there's anything wrong. I already know what I'm going to say; I've given this problem, these melt downs, plenty of thought. I explain that there's nothing actually wrong, right now. I explain that I just seem to be an impossibly sensitive person. I try to briefly explain my theory that my brain is over-firing certain chemicals and so I react more strongly to basic emotional stimuli.

Hannah nods kindly and agrees that that's one way to look at what is happening to me. Then, she suggests that another way to look at it is that I'm a healer, and I'm feeling all of this for the people around me. She suggests that perhaps I'm holding space for others, emotionally, and this is what is overwhelming for me. I nod kindly and silently agree to disagree with this beautiful woman; I'm no nurse. We hug and separate.

Shortly after this, as I walk slowly down a side path in an effort to avoid all of the people who just watched me have a meltdown, one of those people comes around the corner and up the path in front of me. I pause and step out of the way, red eyes to the ground. Ken pauses, and then approaches me slowly. Our eyes connect, and he gently asks me if I'm grieving. I don't know what to say; I'm not grieving. I don't know what I'm doing, I'm just feeling. I have nothing to actually be sad about. I tell him all of this.

Ken looks at me, hard, and asks me if I can talk to animals. This gets my attention. I *can* talk to animals, but this isn't something strangers usually know about me. I tell him that, too. Ken asks me if I've heard the term "empath". This one is new to me. He suggests that, whenever I make it back to the internet, I look it up. We hug and separate.

That night, we all sit for the Ayahuasca ceremony.

*** *** ***

(Oakland, September 2017)

Sitting here looking back, two and a half years after that night, it's as though I'm looking back on two separate lives, with that ceremony being the bridge between the two.

In my previous life, I spent most of my time farming, working with animals because humans were too overwhelming. While kind and friendly, I was, internally, emotionally volatile and I spent a good portion of my time dancing with depression. I thought I might be bipolar. I was also intelligent and well educated, good at my job, and I was able to find sincere joy in the simplest moments. However, ultimately, I was a very sad individual, with the desire to fix a broken world, and the motivation, but without the tools to even handle my own brokenness, much less anyone else's. I landed in that forest in Costa Rica after two solid years of depression. When I landed there, I really did expect that I would just be miserable for the rest of my life; that was just the hand that I was dealt.

But, there was still a part of me that just could not abide this (I expect it's the part of me that got me to Costa Rica that year). I could not be expected to persist in misery - how is this possible? I had been happy before; it must be possible to do that again, somehow.

After seriously considering, and then deciding against pharmaceutical solutions, I turned back yet again to myself. I'd gotten myself out of this before. (Before: the last time I'd been depressed, when I'd just buckled down and explored mental conditioning and mantras in order to employ self-developed Pavlovian psychological training techniques to rewire my brain out of depression). This time, I involved a larger community in my healing process by seeking help from ayahuasca and the wonderful souls who are working with it, and that has allowed for the next stage of my growth.

I've realized a lot since then.
I've realized that Hannah was right; I am a healer.
I've realized that Ken was right; I am empathic.
And, I've realized that I was right; my brain is a bit weird.

All of this is coming together for me these days, as I try to figure out what exactly it is that I should be doing here on this planet, as I live a more beautiful life than I ever could have anticipated or thought to ask for.

*** *** ***

(Ocean City, Fall 2015)

It's late at night. The room is dark, and I can't sleep. I squirm under the weight of Mike's leg; I can't sleep, but I try to be still, in case he's managed it. I listen for his breathing, and when I realise that he's lying awake next to me, I can no longer contain myself. "I can't sleep. I'm so insecure right now."

These words burst out, unbidden, before I can stop them. This is a habit of mine - an intentional one - I say my negative emotions. Out loud. To someone. I've found that this is, generally, about 80% of the battle. But, I also try not to do that after a long night of drunken admissions as I lay beside the incredibly sweet, incredibly messed up man who made those admissions.

Without missing a beat, Mike replies, "Oh my god, me too."

The meaning of the moment sinks into my mind. I pause, and then I answer him. "Hmm, okay. Let's talk about why you're feeling insecure."

We're both asleep within minutes.

*** *** ***

(Oakland, August 2017)

I think a lot these days about that night in Mike's bed - the first time I was aware of feeling a specific emotion for a specific person. The thing is, I was aware of feeling it for someone else because I had put so much effort into just being able to say the feeling out loud for myself. And, there's so much to unpack in that one little fact.

There's another memory I'll never forget - the first time Erin told me she was feeling grumpy; the morning Erin gave me the tool that I needed to be able to face my emotions.

It was a fresh summer morning in the foothills in Colorado, and we were probably on our way to breakfast or some such. Erin and I were working together at a summer camp for kids, and this morning was early in both the summer and our friendship. As we walked along, still enjoying the peace and quiet of the morning, Erin said, unprompted, "I'm feeling grumpy today".

Taken aback, I looked at her with concern and apologised that she was feeling this way. Without missing a beat, Erin assured me that I had no reason to apologise - she wasn't saying that I made her grumpy. She just wanted to let me know she was feeling grumpy, just in case she acted grumpy. She wanted me to know that any negative behavior from her was a reflection of her internal state, not of anything I had done.

I was, again, taken aback - but on an entirely different level. You could do this? Identify negative emotions *before* they explode out of you? Share your experience with others so that you didn't accidentally hurt them? What?

This conversation happened back in 2009, just after I graduated from college. I didn't know what it was at the time, but I had been dealing with depression - on and off - for at least a couple years at this point. Part of not knowing I was depressed, I realise now, was tied into my inability to express any negative emotions before they exploded out of me. And even then, during the explosions (which looked remarkably more like meltdowns than explosions), I was generally as confused as anyone else as to what was actually wrong with me.

Erin offered me a way out of this madness; I could try just saying how I felt. What a novel concept.

So, I started trying to figure out how I felt. I started practicing saying my negative feelings out loud. I told anyone who was around me, and I'm sure I made more than a few people uncomfortable. But, something inside me had snapped, and I doubt anyone could have stopped the deluge once these emotions started pouring out of me.

Once I started learning how to really express myself, something else started to happen - I started to come to terms with my sadness, this sadness that had landed so heavy on top of me, so long ago. I started to realise that my sadness was dynamic and shifting - in other words, I started to learn that my sadness wasn't permanent. And, I started to pay attention to when I felt what kinds of sadness.

And then, another really big thing started happening - I started to feel better. Somehow, all of those sad feelings that used to smother me until they exploded/melted out of me, well, I guess I started to work through them. Literally. For so long, I had shoved every single bad feeling that I had deep down inside of myself, because I didn't realise you were ever allowed to feel bad. Now, I realised that saying these feelings seemed to be the way to get them out, before they could start to smother me. It was, in a word or two, life changing.

*** *** ***

(Redondo Beach, September 2017)

Jen and I stroll along the street, basking in the late afternoon Californian sun. The noise of the traffic beside us interrupts our conversation briefly, and we head for a side street so that we can stop trying to talk over it.

I just got down to LA this morning, and we've been wandering and chatting all day, trying to catch each other up on our separate lives as of late. For me, specifically, I'm trying to explain everything that I've been learning and realising and trying to talk to other people about. Suddenly, as the point of everything I've been trying to express coalesces in my mind, I stop in my tracks and realise that this is it; I think I can finally sum it up.

So, here goes...

I've been empathic my entire life. My entire life, I've felt everyone else's pain *with* them. For years, I had no clue that this is why I had been so incredibly sad.

This sadness has allowed me so many vast and varied opportunities for personal growth. I've learned how to acknowledge my emotions honestly, and without shame. I've learned how to sit beside my own pain, and not need to suffer from it. And the practice of learning to say my own sadnesses has morphed into the practice of me helping other people say their own sadnesses.

Learning how to express my emotions - negative and positive - has provided me with the tools to examine those emotions. For us humans, so much of recovering from, or getting past, our emotional lives and our feelings is just *identifying* those emotions and feelings. *Really* identifying them; honestly, and without shame. Only then can you look at yourself compassionately and ask genuinely what you might really be needing from yourself and others - why that emotion might have sprung into existence.

So often, the emotions that we find on the surface of our experience are secondary or even tertiary responses to a more specific need; one that we have been trained by society to deny.

Here's the thing about our lives here, as these painfully aware and conscious animals - our lives are not our own. We are slaves to our instincts and our bodies, whether or not we ever realise that fact, and so we spend so much of our time just trying to survive our animal instinct to survive. The reason that we have so much trouble with this is because our current social structure requires us to deny our animal selves. And so, the only option for our animal self (being told by instinct that it needs to fit in - don't get kicked out of the pack or you'll starve/be eaten), is to deny itself.

What's more, our current culture requires complicity in the forms of the repression it enacts on us. The animal instinct to get along with packmates - to be part of a community - is predated upon, morphed into this compelling need to be just like everyone else. But, here's the thing - we aren't all just like each other. Every single one of us is unique. We each contain multitudes of galaxies within ourselves; anyone who has ever had an experience with psychedelic drugs can attest to that fact. And yet, the narrative that we live within is that we should all be exactly the same, and any delineation from the norm is cause for suspicion, if not murder. We are taught to wear masks to hide our differences, and anyone who dares to show their most vulnerable self is the "different" one.

And so, we walk around as truncated versions of ourselves; we walk around wearing the masks that society straps on us, slowly cracking apart inside because it is so painful to deny so much of ourselves all of the time. It is this pain that leads to the cognitive dissonance that allows us to participate in our own repression.

I've stopped being complicit in my own repression.

Instead, these days I actively work to address the cognitive dissonance that I have inevitably found installed in myself. I work to ask myself about why I might be feeling the feelings I feel, and whether the why is based in the reality that I'm currently existing in, or instead, in some impossible reality that I have been conditioned to believe in. I think about what, besides the most honest expression of my true, kind self, might be influencing the ways that I'm responding to the world around me.

This brings me back to motivations. Our responses to our experiences are motivated by so many different things. Our behaviour is shaped by our physical bodies, and their physiology at any given time. An interesting study led by Shai Danzinger of Ben-Gurion University looked at judges presiding over parole hearings in Israel, and it suggests that such a basic thing as our blood sugar actively shapes our largest philosophical and moral decisions. When we are tired or stressed, our complex reasoning suffers as our brain becomes focused on a fight or flight response to our modern world. Conversely, we can recover from a fight or flight response by counting by threes to engage our prefrontal lobe in our mental conversation; so much of how we act is subjective to how we are thinking.

Then, there are other things that drive the ways we behave. There are our animal instincts; all of the basic ways that our brain was built to work so that we could survive in the caves and forests before central heating and indoor plumbing. There is the instinct to fit in, to be a contributing part of the pack, or the community. And, the instinct to protect yourself from pain. There is the instinct to mistrust change, and to avoid that which might upset the status quo.

In considering all of this, remember, if you will, that our animal brains are not charged with ensuring happy, emotionally fulfilled lives, but rather survival. Our animal brains would much rather ensure survival as completely as possible, rather than making sure that our lives are worth surviving.

Another thing that affects our behaviour is the actual, current structure of our brain. As dynamic as our brains are, and as malleable and capable of change as they are, at any given time, any given brain is locked in a set of chemically controlled impulses and charges, swirling about in a fairly measured, structured dance. Our habitual patterns, the Pavlovian foundations for our daily existence, inherently influence our daily existence. And so, the patterns of behaviour that we learn to mimic from our very earliest time here come to define us. Our behaviour becomes, to an extent, predetermined (as distasteful as this is for so many of us to admit).

With all of this in mind, let's discuss cognitive dissonance. In my mind, I always see cognitive dissonance as a wall. To me, it is a solid structure erected between two conflicting parts of our brain. The sole purpose of this wall is to obstruct the view between those two parts of the brain- to avoid the introspection necessary to realize that you are holding two competing ideas at once.

Our brains do this in an effort to protect us, but- again- it is important to remember that the brain is tasked with survival in the wild, not a holistically healthy experience in the context of modern society.

As an empath, it has been especially important that I learn how to address my own emotions, and my own cognitive dissonance. This is because, so often, what I'm feeling isn't my own emotion, but rather some version of someone else's emotion. However, it's impossible to even begin considering this until I consider what my own emotions might feel like and mean. To find out what my emotions might mean, I am usually required to unearth and sort through some cognitive dissonance.

And so, I think a lot about motivations these days. I think about physiology and instinct and society, and I think about our most basic, most authentically needy selves. Nearly always, I've found that nearly any given behavior is motivated by a number of these factors, in varying degrees and varying ways. Nonetheless, if I can follow the cognitive dissonance that I become aware of back to the motivations of that cognitive dissonance, I can generally undermine the foundation of that cognitive dissonance- being able to see the ways that your brain is lying to itself generally precludes your brain lying to itself.

And once you can stop your brain lying to itself, you can participate more fully in your brain- and subsequently the rest of you- living a fuller, more authentic life. You can participate in performing your own emotional work, and along the way you can learn how to emotionally support yourself. This is, essentially, learning how to meet your own needs, emotionally and otherwise.

And once you're capable of meeting your own needs, it becomes immensely easy to be there for others, and to help them learn how to meet their own needs.

And if it's the denial of our basic needs that lies at the center of all of our conflict, then perhaps this is the beginning of how we start creating a more peaceful world.

So, I invite you to join me; I invite you to consider listening more carefully to yourself, and to the people around you. I invite you to question your motivations, and why you act the way that you do. And I invite you to approach yourself and others with kindness and compassion and a willingness to understand and forgive.

I invite you to be vulnerable, despite the inherent risk in vulnerability. And I invite you to speak up for yourself, and to take care of yourself, and to love yourself unconditionally.

I invite you to rest in the knowledge that imperfections are inherent in our experience, and that the beauty of the world can be found in its imperfections. And I invite you to bask in your exploration of your own imperfections- all of these wonderful opportunities to discover a deeper layer of our experience.

It is my sincere hope that we can all work together to more compassionately understand our own experience and the experiences of those around us. From there, who knows what we could accomplish?

Frannie

A Magic Kind of Normal

Jo-Anne Brown

H ave you ever felt like everyone around you is looking at you; analysing and criticising every detail of who you are? Like you're so uncomfortable that it's hard to breathe? Have you ended up physically exhausted after a day around a large group of people? Felt overwhelmed while going to a shopping centre, especially places with lots of people? You might find a certain person in your life who physically drains you so much, it's like they're sucking out all your energy leaving you mentally and physically exhausted every time you catch up. How about all the above?

This has been my daily experience for all of my life. I feel and experience day to day experiences, not only in my own life, but I also feel the emotions, thoughts, moods and worries of the people around me on an unusually strong level. The easiest way to describe it is that I feel peoples 'stuff' emotionally and at times, physically. It doesn't matter whether I know the person or have just met them for the first time. Stuff seems to get to me more easily than everyone else. It happens with everyone I encounter - friends, family, work colleagues - and even strangers that I have just met.

I've always been known as the emotional, mothering type in my circle of friends. I can't even begin to imagine just how many times I've heard, "you're too sensitive", or "you're too emotional" during my lifetime.

Ever since I can remember, I have felt different from most of the people I have come to know throughout my journey. I always knew there was something about life that I saw and felt that others didn't. I just didn't have a name for it, or a way to describe it. I spent most of my younger life confused because it's hard enough processing your own feelings in life, without taking on the feelings of other people as well. I sometimes feel like I'm walking around with a heart that's like a sponge; absorbing everyone else's emotional and energetic burdens. At times, I feel it physically as well. Sometimes, it was like I had a physical weight on my shoulders; an overwhelming heaviness that was hard to explain to anyone; at least logically. So, if I say, "I feel your pain", or "I understand more than you know", I literally mean what I say.

When I was growing up, anything that didn't fit into what was viewed as 'normal' or 'socially acceptable' was laughed at or ridiculed. Thankfully, people are now more open minded around ideas and suggestions that can't be scientifically proven. Society now looks at the unknown differently, and it's common to consider all possibilities without proven evidence.

Until I was in my late twenties, I had become confident in the fact that I was completely different, and no one would ever understand the real me. I never thought I'd find anyone who understood the extreme emotional roller coaster of life that I ride daily. At twenty-seven, I began questioning my perception and understanding of the world. I asked the question, "Surely I can't be the only proud weirdo in the world?"

So, my journey began. I researched and absorbed as much as I possibly could. I joined support groups. I looked for and met people online who understood what I go through every day, because they go through the same thing! This was when I came to learn of a group of special people called Empaths. The only way to describe it is that I had finally found myself. I finally understood that the confusing way I view the world, was normal and not as crazy as the 'reality' that I had been led to believe was fact. Finally, it all made sense. I AM AN EMPATH!

In that moment, I knew that my life would change forever. I'd found me. I made the joyous realisation that all the unexplained and confusing feelings *finally* had meaning! My mind opened to a whole new world that for the first time in my life, felt whole. My thirst for knowledge didn't end; I just became a bigger sponge! It wasn't just that I was absorbing emotion, but it was the wealth of knowledge I had discovered, which brought understanding to what had always been so bewildering to me. My world blossomed.

One of the biggest lessons I learned was about energy and how it is at the base of everything in life. Especially how much of an effect energy can have on emotions, people, places, even ourselves. Being empathic, energy - both positive and negative - play a huge part in life. That's why for empathic people, energy protection is so important, because we're more susceptible to absorbing negative energy. I had to learn to block others' energies and emotions from having an effect on my own personal feelings. As an empath, this is one of the first things I would encourage other empaths to focus on mastering. The other, which is imperative, is being able to release negative energy. As empaths, we are beacons of light that attract negative energy. We're easy targets. That's why releasing negativity is so important. My favourite way of doing this is to have a shower and let all the negativity run down the plug hole! Meditation is also brilliant, as it creates focus on bringing us back to the positive. If you are or know an empathic person, you'll notice that they can carry stress if their self-care is neglected.

After a lot of practice, I started dealing with stressful situations by taking a step back when things get too much. And, it works! Even separating yourself for a moment makes all the difference, by using that moment to take a breath, recollect and reset your boundaries. A great deal of the time, this helps and

I'm back, ready to face whatever
way!

Despite what some people say, we
too sensitive or *too* emotional; we
with our emotions better than m
understand and relate to what oth
well. In saying that, we aren't all superheroes with
negative fighting super powers. Learn to trust your
gut feelings.

One of the perks of being empathic is that you
become very in tune with your intuition. One way to
look at it, is that empathic people are like walking lie
detectors! Basically, if something doesn't feel right,
listen. Trust what you 'just know' intuitively. When I
feel, I don't only feel emotion. It's a bunch of layers
that make up the way I see things. Emotions are so
strong, that it's like there is a shift or weight in the
air. The energy has a warmth or coolness to it.
Everything in which a person expresses themselves
comes into the way I experience 'them'. I see the
persona that someone radiates. I see all of this, even
before the person has said one word.

After hearing lots of other empathic people's stories,
one thing I've noticed is that empaths make great
friends! Well, at least I like to think so! Maybe it's
because we understand people on another level, and
its second nature to put yourself in someone else's
shoes. Another common trait that I have noticed with
every empathic person I've met is that they are
honest and loyal. Loyalty is huge!

to only surround myself with people I know I can trust. During my lifetime, I have been betrayed more times than I can count, mostly because I have a kind nature and look for the good in people regardless of first impressions. Unfortunately, this can be to my detriment. As a loyal, kind and generous friend by nature, I think I have a right to expect the same kind of honesty, loyalty and genuine friendship in return.

As you get older and experience life, you undeniably learn lessons from the different paths that you take. As a result, learning the hard way by naively trusting the wrong people, I now distance myself from selfish, rude and toxic people. People like that make me want to run a mile! I also absolutely detest narcissism! I cannot get my head around how a narcissist thinks. It's the exact opposite of everything that makes up my core beliefs of how people should be treated.

After living life 'in the knowing' for almost ten years, I'm able to adapt my life to certain situations that 'normal' people may not have an issue with. It's not that I am constantly walking on eggshells, expecting to fall apart at the slightest show of emotion, it's just that I approach situations differently to most. I have to consider the emotional side, as well as all the other factors of everyday life.

Some might ask, "wouldn't it just be easier to turn off your feelings and act unemotionally?" That is an answer I will never know. This is me. Wonderful, glorious, amazing, special and spectacular me!

In conclusion, as empaths, we know what you are going through because we are going through it with you.

"It's not that you're abnormal; you're a magic kind of normal!"

JoAnne

From Troubled Empath to Liberated Warrior

Jo Nicholls

All of my life I have been an empath, but like many others, I had no idea what the childhood labels of being shy, quiet, over sensitive, withdrawn or emotional meant. It is a common story – empaths have felt misunderstood, different or alienated from others around them all their lives until they learned or realised why. The realisation may have come from meeting another like them, reading something they could relate to, finding themselves in a situation where things got recurrently messy, or when things naturally began to fall into place.

My own awareness of being an empath came when my spiritual path became clearer, after years of feeling lost in the fog of overpowering feelings. I know how it feels to wonder if you are crazy or to question why you do not understand other people. I know what it is to become a recluse, to avoid social interactions and to make excuses to friends in order to avoid being around other people, and then being overwhelmed by the guilt of doing so. For some time, I felt that the more I learnt and experienced, the more I realised that the problem was that certain people or situations would either drain or recharge my energy; this led to me blaming others for depleting my energy.

Fortunately, curiosity has always been one of my strongest traits and I have never shied away from self-reflection or from taking personal responsibility for my choices. Rather than continuing to feel overpowered by the energies around me, I began a journey of self-exploration to take control of my spiraling emotions and energy.

In the decade since then, I have learnt what an empath is, and how to balance those energies to maintain my health; in turn I support others to do the same. I have learnt that an empath's journey into emotional health depends on five key areas, which I think it will be helpful to share:

1 - Knowledge: You must seek and embrace higher knowledge related to metaphysical principles of past life, soul contracts, soul wounds, self-sabotage and blockages, using development circles and more.

2 - Awareness: You must be aware of yourself and others as an observer, rather than a judge. The initiative is to gain insights about YOU as you monitor your thoughts, words, actions, reactions and feelings. The ability to gather these insights about yourself and others will help your growth and the way that you interact with others tremendously.

3 - Energy Skills: You must learn about energetic connections in the world and within yourself. Your awareness combined with energy skills, helps you understand how you are affected by energy. You will learn resilience and healthy energy regulating tools related to yourself as an energetic being.

4 - Intuitive Development: You will be connecting to your guidance, to understand the world in a new way. You will learn to trust, love and gain enough confidence to accept and embrace your inner knowing.

5 - Self-Healing: Your number one directive is to be courageous and step into self-healing. This involves transmuting and transcending the denser energies affecting you mentally, emotionally, spiritually and physically. Only by stepping away from the blame of others, does lasting healing occur. It takes great strength and desire to break through, to let go of victim status. If you do persevere in this though, you will learn resilience; finding balance and peace.

Many people, especially those with an interest in healing, use the label of 'empath' like a trophy - to describe a gift, a skill, a reason that they are more in tune with, or better able to help others. All too often it becomes an excuse for judging others and not taking responsibility for regulating their own energy fields, as I learned to do. Instead, a prison of denial, avoidance and blame is created, leading to empaths having volatile relationships with the people around them. For me, it is clear: unless you learn to regulate your energy field, it will become a subconscious anchor holding you back from evolving into your truest self.

These insights I share with others were not always clear to me, but have come from a decade of growth, of living, studying, making mistakes and learning from them. If I see others lost in a similar fog, prey to strong emotions and confusing impressions, I offer my own experience as a landmark, knowing that our paths may be different, but that there are many common pitfalls on the route to becoming a balanced empath. Ego is definitely one of them, and self-awareness is key in avoiding that particular pitfall.

In my energy and counselling work with others, one way I stay balanced is to make sure I have regular peer support sessions, where I practice setting bias aside in order to learn and grow. In one of these sessions, I was given a very important label and told to look up what a Heyoka Empath was. As soon as I read the description, I had a light bulb moment and suddenly many things seemed to fall into place!

A Heyoka is the rarest form of empath and it is the least understood and the most feared. This is because of the very powerful lessons it forces upon you. It is the ultimate mirror of self: you will see within the Heyoka, the darkest side of yourself, often hidden and denied, on which you need to work. Those coming from a place of love see this within you and gain reassurance of their path, but those with many lessons ahead of them and coming from a place of anger, guilt or resentment will see in you things that they have long denied exist within themselves - which is not always an easy lesson to accept or learn.

In Native American tribes where they were respected and revered for their abilities, Heyokas would be the ones to open people's eyes to new possibilities and different aspects of a situation. They were recognised as being the holders of chaos medicine, because while it can be an unsettling and vulnerable experience meeting a Heyoka, its disruption would never be meant to harm or destroy.

The Heyoka enables the humblest to see the mirror of truth and themselves as they authentically are. Their ability to know the cause of a situation is often daunting and only those who have developed their intuition enough to receive this lesson, will acknowledge it. Furthermore, the Heyoka empath also has the ability to shift the energy of a group, through their understanding of emotions and so are often healers, mediators or therapists in modern day societies. Heyokas help people who are disheartened or stuck, to see that there is more than one path in life. They are able to look at a situation from outside the box and from back to front. They see alternative routes and how to do some things backwards. They have an innate ability to change people's lives in a single meeting by bringing them outside of society's one-track way of thinking, thus opening new doors and removing old blockages.

Heyokas rarely tell others of their power, which is the part of my extensive research that has stuck with me the most. I have learnt not to focus on this label, but to accept that with it comes great responsibility. I simply use it to understand my own interactions, humbly accepting that energy has no boundaries, so is difficult to define let alone change. Here, writing about the empath's journey, I am sharing my experiences and lessons to help others to become free, if that is part of their journey.

Regardless of the type of empath you believe that you are, I have learnt that just as an empty cup cannot fill another, an unbalanced empath cannot help others.

This is where the term of 'energy vampire' comes from. I have been one, and over the years have also met many. Energy vampires are unbalanced empaths, who are often unaware of this, as they describe other people as draining their energy and sucking them dry. Actually, this is the result of them not being able to recharge themselves from the other person - if perhaps their energy too is erratic. If two energy sources are depleted and are trying to recharge solely from each other, they will naturally become burnt out, drained and exhausted just from trying. What they are recognising is in fact, energy similar to their own. It is only when an energy vampire is around those with better balanced energy that they begin to feel better. What they do not realise or perhaps acknowledge, is that they are, in fact, feeling better because it is them doing the draining. Having discussed this issue with many good friends and acquaintances who are empaths, there seems to be a consensus that the way to become healthy energetically is to focus on your personal development. In doing so, in exploring who and what you are, you will find your own unique self-reliant recharging tool. Mine happens to be my garden - a sanctuary - just spending time there recharges my batteries. This allows me to explore the world without affecting those around me, and it keeps me secure in the knowledge that I am able to put myself back on charge at any time.

Being an empath is not a gift and it is not a trophy. It is not a curse and it does not make you any different to anyone else. Being aware of your own unique energy is something everyone - declared empath or not - would benefit from working towards. If the energy you are surrounded with makes you unhappy or sick, then you have the power to change that. What I teach, is that nobody need live in unhealthy conditions, not even empaths. We are all beautiful, energetic beings here to learn, share and grow in order to evolve. As we evolve, our intuition and its connection to source strengthens.

If you are reading this and have found yourself locked into this title of empath, begin by loving yourself, and from there, humility and acceptance will put you hand in hand with your connection to your highest self - your intuition - and this will show you the way forwards as a true warrior.

Jo

Always Healing

Justine Luzzi

I always knew I was different, but I wasn't sure how or why. I always realised I took things a bit more seriously, was overly sensitive, had a really difficult time with balance, and was way more intuitive than my counterparts.

Around twenty-eight years old, I had a spiritual awakening (more specifically, a Kundalini awakening) that was so sudden and intense, I considered checking myself into a mental institution on more than one occasion. This awakening was triggered by the rock bottom I had hit. I was coming out of a toxic, narcissistic abusive relationship, as well as dealing with the repercussions of my DUI charge.

For months, I was drinking heavily to ensure I couldn't feel any of my feelings; shame, guilt, hating myself, my broken heart, and every other feeling I've never dealt with. And as empath, not only do you have your own feelings, you can easily absorb others'. So, in retrospect, I was trying to drown out all of that. When I finally changed my environment and quit the drinking, and adopted healthier habits like yoga and meditation, that's when the spiritual awakening began.

I went to Catholic school for eight years of my life. I just remember going to church on a weekly basis and not feeling a connection to religion at all. As soon as I entered public high school, I deemed myself an atheist and kept that identity for thirteen years of my life. What I realise now, was that being an atheist was a direct rebellion against religion in general, and not what I truly believed. All along I was a spiritual being, just like the rest of us. After all, we are all spiritual beings having a human experience, not the other way around.

I remember feeling very lonely because all I wanted to do was explore spirituality, learn to heal myself holistically, and figure out these special intuitive gifts that I became conscious of during this awakening. I had absolutely no one in my life that could understand me. I know a lot of people say that social media is destroying our relationships, but if it wasn't for social media, I wouldn't have been able to connect to like-minded people. Everyone just wants to be loved and understood; it's a basic need. I found Facebook groups dedicated to spirituality and ultimately, empaths.

That was the first time I had heard the word. Without even knowing what it was, I resonated with it deeply. It was like the clouds parted, and I figured myself out. My whole life, I had wondered why people don't feel the way I do, that something was wrong with me because I couldn't just 'get over it', let go, and move on as swiftly as other people. I always needed tremendous alone time and I processed my emotions more deeply and intricately than others. I always had to go the extra mile to protect my energy. Figuring out I was an empath turned out to be part of the healing process. I was able to understand that being compassionate to myself during healing, was healing in itself.

As an empath, not only do you feel things very deeply, but you have special intuitive gifts that come along with it. I discovered those gifts in full force during my awakening, and it truly scared me to no end.

I have claircognizance (clear knowing) and clairsentience (clear feeling). These are extra-sensory gifts where there are things I just know and feel to be true. So, during my awakening when I became conscious, I became conscious of not just the feelings I wasn't feeling, but also things that didn't even exist in this dimension. Hence, my desire to check myself into a mental institution.

That had to be the hardest part for me, and still continues to be. A lot of empaths have grown up being conscious of their gifts, but I only became aware of mine at twenty-eight years old. So, that means for all those years I was used to an on-the-surface life. And now all of a sudden, metaphysics were real and affecting my life very deeply.

I still struggle with this. The mind is actually controlled by the ego, which is very logical. So, we are trained to believe it when we see it. When in reality, if we can believe it, we can see it. To be transparent, the fear of caring what other people think about me has been what has really been holding me back. But, I continue to work with mentors to expand my gifts and work with fear-clearing exercises as well. I have gone into professional spiritual life coaching and mentor highly sensitive people and empaths on how to manage their emotions in a world that is difficult to live in. I also run a meet up group in New York City.

The journey really has been a healing one and has helped me to identify my higher self and true purpose in this world. I truly am a healer and make strides every day to utilise my gift. If you're an empath, you know the struggles of your sensitivity. But in all honesty, your sensitivity is not a curse, it's a gift. Empaths are light workers; souls whose true purpose is to bring light to the dark and help others to recognise that we are all one, and that love is the only thing that's real.

Justine

Feeling my way below the surface

Leah Moffitt

An empath's journey is an epic exploration of the inner world, where feelings dominate and you are drawn to the undercurrents bubbling below the surface of life. At times, you can feel as though you are drowning in unrelenting waves of emotions that threaten to consume you, leaving you unable to discern which feelings are your own. Then, there are times when you touch people's hearts with your immense capacity for compassion and love. Although I have experienced most of the traits of an empath for as long as I can remember, I hadn't really come across much information about it until recently. Yet, everything I have discovered resonates with me strongly, and now

I consider being an empath more of a blessing, rather than a curse.

I have always thought that there was more to life than just what we see. When I was around four years old, my dad told my brother and I that everyone had guardian angels looking after them. I was both fascinated and comforted by the idea that there were loving beings I could not see watching over me. From that day, I have always called upon the angels and God to guide and support me through life, and my prayers have always been answered in one way or another. So-called 'coincidences' have been a natural part of my life, but I am still in total awe and gratitude of the wonderful ways the universe works. Often, what you think you want is not always what you need, and I've come to accept that in life, the most difficult challenges are the best opportunities for growth. I am a dreamer and thrive on a strong element of the mystical, which has proven to be a lifesaving source of hope when I've been on a downward spiral.

I was always told I was 'too sensitive' or 'moody' when, in reality, I was a sponge soaking up the (often negative) energy in my environment. For much of my early life, I fell victim to the energies around me and felt powerless to gain control over these consuming feelings. I would suddenly be overcome by sadness or burning with rage, with no idea where it all came from. Crowds would leave me frazzled, exhausted and moody. I remember looking at strangers and starting to sob as I would see glimpses of their life and sense their sadness as if it were my own. Sometimes in new places, I would get a sense of déjà vu and it would take a long time to shake strange feelings of being in another time, another place and another person's shoes. It might sound extreme, but that is how life can be for an empath – life lessons are emotionally amplified and what feels like the entire spectrum of the emotional scale is experienced at some time or another.

When I entered my teenage years, my sensitivity heightened, and my emotions were amplified tenfold. I often felt depressed, lonely and at times suicidal as I was desperate to break free from the web of feelings that kept me constantly entangled. When I was fourteen, it was like the psychic floodgates flung open.

I began hearing voices, seeing apparitions, having premonitions and lucid dreaming. I thought I was going crazy.

Thankfully, a light appeared at the end of the tunnel at this tumultuous time. Astrology was introduced into my life by one of mother's friends, and I discovered the key that unlocked the door to my soul. My mum and I devoured as many books on the subject as we could and studied our own charts and the placements of those around us. The lightbulb moments just kept flashing. Astrology became second nature and provided me with a much-needed depth. It helped me to define the energies within myself and the people around me. Now, I can easily identify an empath by a strong water element (Cancer, Scorpio or Pisces) in their chart, as these energies relate strongly to the feeling world of an empath.

Even though I had discovered this amazing tool that helped to improve my understanding of people and the cycles of life, I had low self-esteem and still lived much of my life putting the feelings of others before my own; to the point of letting them walk all over me. As an empath, I felt great satisfaction in helping people; however, an empath without boundaries is a magnet for energy vampires – victims, drama queens and narcissists being the most common. I would get drawn into the negativity and drama of these people and was left feeling depleted. I would feel frustrated that I would listen for hours to their problems and give them the advice they asked for, yet they wouldn't do anything to change their situations. They would dump their negativity on me and walk away feeling lighter, leaving me drained and resentful. Before too long, they would return, and I allowed the pattern to repeat. I hated the world, so I shut my feelings off and became very withdrawn. It was a typical survival mechanism for an ill-equipped empath. I started binge drinking as a teen to escape.

For a long time, it felt amazing to get drunk, let go and be one of the crowd, but as time went on, I became angry, mean and depressed each time I drank. My last major binge was in my late twenties when I almost drank an entire bottle of vodka and was so full of rage, I just wanted to smash everything. I scared myself. This wasn't who I was, and I knew it was time to stop.

Empaths who are not aware of how to utilise their gifts or protect themselves often use addictions to numb their feelings.

At twenty-nine, I had a major turning point in my life. In astrology, it's referred to as a Saturn Return and happens to everyone somewhere between the ages of twenty-seven and thirty. This is when you are initiated into 'true' adulthood. If your life hasn't been built on the best of foundations, then it's highly likely aspects of your life may come crashing down in order for you to build new foundations that are more aligned to who you truly are. During my Saturn Return, I lost my job, my relationship, my health was suffering, and I had no place to call home. My whole life was out of alignment. I was angry that I had given so much but ended up with nothing. This situation led me to finally realise that I had tried to squish myself into a 'normal' box and suppress the person I truly was. So, I surrendered and stopped trying to salvage everything around me. My mum realised I was at the end of my rope and drove to Sydney. We threw some belongings into our cars and I followed her back to Melbourne. I felt like I was in a daze, but before I knew it, I was living with my mum and her partner in a new city. Although I was grateful for them taking me in, I felt like a failure and back at square one. I was a mess and could not believe everything had come crashing down around me. But, by having nothing more to lose, I could see the next phase in my life as a clean slate and an opportunity to connect and be my authentic self. I made a very conscious decision to take responsibility for my life, change my way of thinking, and become more aware of my energy.

One significant lesson I've learned as an empath is that it is vital to keep thoughts and feelings in check. Empaths can soak up the most minute vibrations;

both personal and collective. Over the years, I have also found that what I put out, I get back in return, whether it be positive or negative. I spent most of my life dwelling in negativity, and that's what I had mostly received. Visualisation works extremely well for empaths because they can imagine all the finer details of what they want and feel it; giving more power to their thoughts becoming reality. Not long after I moved to Melbourne, I created a vision board of myself, a loving and supportive husband and a baby, and to my delight, they 'materialised' within two years. For the first time in my life, I felt truly happy.

Like most empaths, I have always been a natural counsellor; attracting people needing support and direction on their journey.

Empaths can often be found in caring professions or healing fields and are often very gifted when it comes to forms of divination as they can easily tune in to personal and collective energy. I have always had the ability to look at a person and get an instant snapshot of their personality and a picture of what's going on in their life. I started to get more 'serious' about my gift of insight and read at events and psychic expos. Astrology and tarot are the tools of choice I used to provide further guidance to people needing direction and insight into their journey. It was such a rewarding feeling to connect on a deep level with strangers and have them walk away feeling hope and inspiration. I felt I was in my element.

I was doing readings at a psychic expo the day my dad died. For most of the day, I had felt a strange sensation in the pit of my stomach and was unable to focus. In the afternoon, I got a call from my husband delivering the devastating news. Losing my dad has been the most heart shattering experience of my life and has affected me profoundly. He was the most gentle and wise soul, and one of the few people who understood me. He would often tell me I had spiritual gifts and praise me up, but I thought that as my dad, he was obligated to say nice things. He was always trying to help me see the brightness of my own light and give me the confidence to believe in myself; to get out there and shine. Empaths are often introverts, have great difficulty believing in themselves and can be very modest about their abilities. I know my dad would want me to do what makes me happy and he knew I loved helping people. When I am ready, I will return to this type of work in some form or another.

Empaths need time to retreat; to go within and process life. Certain events such as the death of loved ones, can cause immense emotional upheaval. It is important to be patient with yourself and process all the feelings as they arise. It is unrealistic to be positive all the time; part of honouring yourself is acknowledging and accepting the light and dark within, and it is crucial for an empath to let their true feelings flow, regardless of how painful they may be.

I have found that there are some common themes that tend to occur in an empath's life and over time, I have implemented some valuable practices into my daily life that have helped me to find balance, empowerment and positivity:

Protect and cleanse your energy. Protecting and cleansing your physical body and aura is essential. When I feel overwhelmed by energy in my environment, I visualise myself in a bubble and avoid unnecessary eye contact with strangers. I also like to wear and carry crystals as a form of protection.

I remind myself not to take on other people's 'stuff' and that at the end of the day, they make their own life choices. I have found that since I have worked on lifting my vibration and setting up boundaries, I don't seem to attract the negative situations and people as I had previously.

There are also many cleansing techniques you could try, and it is important to use what resonates with you - some people prefer an elaborate ritual, and others like to keep it simple. The intention is what matters most. Don't forget to declutter and smudge your home regularly.

Grounding is also important, especially if the water element does feature strongly in your astrological chart – getting out into nature is a simple and effective way to ground yourself.

It's okay to say no. This has been the biggest challenge for me, by far. Those close to me know I'm a big softie and that I find it hard to say no. Empaths like to keep the peace and make others happy, often at their own expense. Set boundaries and time limits and avoid harsh environments and abrasive people. People may need you, but you need to stay balanced and keep your energy levels up, or you'll have nothing to give.

Follow your own heart. When you honour yourself, you stand in your own power and gain a stronger sense of self. This helps you to discern your own feelings from those you pick up from others. Empaths can give profound advice, but sometimes have trouble trusting their own intuition as they are often putting the needs of others before their own. Just allow yourself to choose what you truly want to do, rather than what you think will make others happy.

Empaths can pick up mysterious illnesses and pains, so listen to your body. These may well be your own physical ailments but could be the pain of those around you (I am renowned for picking up people's headaches!). Empaths often have strong physical reactions to energy – let these reactions guide you.

Take time out and connect with other empaths. Be clear about the type of people you want to attract, and don't settle for less. Find people who give with love and receive with gratitude. The path of an empath can sometimes be a lonely one, but there are other empaths out there just like you! Put your feelers out and connect. Don't feel guilty if you need to take a break from friendships and relationships now and then – empaths frequently need space and time to decompress. Your empath friends will understand!

No matter how much you think you have it together, there will always be ups and downs in life. Now that I am more aware of what being an empath entails, I am more equipped to deal with the down times and therefore, able to bounce back faster. There are still days when I feel overwhelmed with emotion while watching the news or being in crowds for too long, but I am able to acknowledge these feelings, and distinguish what feelings are my own by quickly using a variety of techniques.

Many empaths are powerful emotional healers and even though it has taken me a long and challenging time to get to this point, I feel blessed to have the gift of insight, the ability to truly empathise, tune right in and to know the right things to say that could heal, change or possibly save a life.

Empaths don't have to share their gifts on a grand scale; they are often the much-needed peacemakers and nurturers within their own family or circle of friends. One thing is for sure; people are drawn to empaths like moths to a flame, and for good reason. They are the listeners, the carers and the healers of this world. Although there can be many challenges along the way, the journey of an empath can be a truly enlightening and rewarding one when you let your bright light shine in this world, and you share your compassionate heart to heal, love and uplift humanity.

Leah

The Pathway to Truth

Maria Solano

As a child, I felt different to my friends. I loved to be social, but was shy, and I had a mentally abusive parent which led to many feelings of low-self-worth. I found I needed regular alone time in my backyard to draw sustenance from nature. I was always reading and wanted to know everything and do everything. I was a very observant child and seemed to know when someone was feeling upset or emotional but was too young to articulate helpful solutions in those instances. I was told later in life that my body took on the emotions of my mother feeling unloved when I was six months old. I couldn't talk, but I could feel, and I did a lot of absorbing.

As I got older, I found people would be drawn to tell me about their lives and problems - friends, strangers on the bus, someone I had just met at a party. I never forgot a face or name. I was drawn to horses, staring at the ocean, going for walks in the bush, collecting crystals, reading tarot cards. I also loved to dance, sing, draw, paint, and write.

I experienced a lot of trauma in childhood and kept having traumatic things happen as the years went by. I had a full-on workload when I could work, and I could never say no to anything. People always came to me to get something done, when they could easily work out how to do it themselves. Much later on, I learnt how to say no, and that led to feelings of emotional strength and confidence. I started to be able to differentiate between mine and others' feelings. I learnt how to not feel guilty for standing up for my feelings, and not taking on board too much, as I could easily get overwhelmed.

I was diagnosed with chronic fatigue syndrome and fibromyalgia at twenty-five years old. This is when I turned even more to my spiritual path. I would attend a metaphysics course for two hours once a week, where we would go through each chakra and associated emotions, and I did a reiki course to try and help self-heal my aches and pains. I tried many other therapies, and even had an EMF expert come out to my house and dowse for draining energy hot spots. At that time, I thought it was the environment draining me, not people.

I would find when I was extremely stressed, light bulbs at home would blow, and most of the battery power in my remotes would drain. Twice when I visited my parent's house, with all the residual anger I was feeling from the mental and emotional abuse, I 'blew' up their TV.

I eventually had to give up work eleven years ago when my CFS became completely overwhelming. I never was a good sleeper, which I think was from learning to be hyper vigilant from childhood, which also lead to anxiety. I would also have about five to six dreams a night, which I would remember vividly and kept a dream journal and a daily journal from when I became a teenager. This I could pour my emotions into and pass them onto the printed page and away from my soul.

As I researched and studied over the years, I came across a Lightworker page where someone had posted about empaths. I downloaded "You're an Empath...... Now What?", and my life up until now started to make complete sense. Feeling different to everyone else, the emotions I would feel that didn't connect to me, the need to know everything, to experience everything, to be in nature, even the CFS all made sense, and my life path became a lot clearer.

I feel like I am starting to head down the right path for my soul's purpose. Learning that I was an empath helped to point me in the right direction of how to live my life without having to be an emotional sponge. I have done a lot of self-development work over the years to learn to value myself, to increase my feelings of self-worth, to gain that confidence to go forth and live my life, my truth, my purpose. I'm learning the right tools to be able to manage my energy, protect myself from other's energy, create clear boundaries and create a serene, positive life, instead of a chaotic, low-energy one.

Being an empath means I feel others' emotions clearly (physically and emotionally) to the point where I can help people face demons that they are either not aware, of or don't want to face. It means bringing light to myself and those who reside in darkness. It can bring sorrow, as I'm attracted to narcissists or people who are intent on destroying themselves, but it can also bring joy as I learn to improve my skills and understanding as an empath, which makes me more self-aware, confident, compassionate and loving.

People and animals tend to be drawn to me, and as I have grown older, I am drawn to meditation, personal development, creativity, and a thirst for knowledge. Meditation in particular helps with the emotions I feel from others - to breathe through the feelings and wash them away at the end of the day - seeing the water as a bright, pure light that transcends all emotions, pain, and suffering, where I can be made whole again.

Watching the news is a struggle - to witness destruction and tragedy – but I also possess a resilience that defies my sensitive heart.

Being an empath has served me well in relationships and employment; knowing what someone needs before they do and knowing what needs to be done before being asked. It has also drained me when allowing others to manipulate my empathy, and inherent kindness and goodness.

I plan to open up a holistic guesthouse. I would love to provide a haven for people who need healing. A space with a Zen garden, juice bar, catering to food allergies, a meditation space, a library, health talks; to help every guest walk away feeling that they are special, appreciated, and important. It would be a place to soothe the soul for people who might need some guidance on their path, or just some rest. I feel I am here to mentor and heal (myself and others).

I come from a place where I have seen the dark but have tried to stay strong in the light.

I was recently chosen to complete a scholarship through an empathy academy, which helped me understand that being an empath is a gift that can be honed to help myself and others. I can help other empaths learn how to protect themselves from negative energy, appreciate and understand their gift and to see it as a positive, enriching part of themselves that they don't have to fear. They can learn how to manage their emotions and use their gifts to build on their own lives to grow; to move forward, to become extraordinary, to provide hope to themselves and others.

Some practices I have used since I learned of becoming an empath to make life easier are:

- When I wake up in the morning, I put a golden bubble around myself for protection.
- Through mindfulness and meditation, I have learnt to be in the present moment, which has

made it easier for me to differentiate between my feelings and others.

- Spending time in nature to nurture, and utilising water to wash away all negativity.
- It's okay to say no. The world won't end. People will still like you. If they have a problem with it, that's their issue, not yours.
- I don't watch the news anymore.
- I have read a lot of articles on empaths, lightworkers, and joined support pages on Facebook to connect with like-minded individuals. We can all help each other evolve and use our gifts in a way that won't drain us, but help ourselves primarily, and then help others to shine their lights, and increase their sparkle.

Maria

Inextricably Linked

Michelle George

I cannot remember a time in my life when I was not keenly aware of how others were feeling, even as a very young child. I grew up in a family who were not (and, are still not) in touch with their emotions or comfortable with expressing emotion, but I always 'knew'. At the age of three, my life changed. My father left, my mother fell apart, and I felt and absorbed her pain as well as my own.

This was something that I was to continue to do, with both my loved ones and strangers throughout my life, as I did not understand the difference between what was 'mine' and what was 'someone else's'. My mother remarried and being an empath became my lifeline. My stepdad was bipolar and his presence in my life was both a challenge and a gift. I became

141

intensely attuned to how he was feeling and was able to predict his reactions. I knew when it was safe to be seen and when to withdraw, seeking the solitude of my room or freedom in the back yard. I knew when to feign sleep, squeezing my eyes shut so tightly and trying to hold my breath to avoid being drawn into conflict. I didn't know how I 'knew' or what label others would give me later on, but I never doubted what I felt.

Picking up on the energy of others was something that became as natural as breathing. This did not always make for an easy life - particularly in my late teens and twenties - and there were times when I wished I could somehow turn it off. In my teens and throughout my twenties, I was often called 'too sensitive' or 'too emotional'. Unaware, I absorbed everything - until all I could feel was pain. I was seen as a pushover, and my compassionate nature meant that I often attracted those who took advantage of my sensitivity. At a time when I was developing a sense of self, my self-concept took repeated blows. I felt like I was in a boat awash at sea, at the mercy of the waves throughout my twenties. I did not have anyone to help me to navigate the seas; to understand what I was feeling.

They say that when the student is ready, the teacher appears and that was certainly the case. I embarked on a period of introspection and self-study. I was introduced to individuals who would help me to understand energy and metaphysical matters. I came to understand that I was indeed an 'empath' and that so much of what I felt was not mine. I cannot tell you how liberating it was to make that realisation. I learned how to distinguish between what was mine and what belonged to others. My greatest teacher has been my husband, who provided me with opportunities to know myself better and put healthy, energetic boundaries into place. I went from someone whose state was determined by that of another, to being able to stand in my own truth, and use what I felt to help others.

I came to value and trust that this precious gift was one that I could use to help others.

It has been said: "It is both a blessing and a curse to feel everything so deeply", but I don't see it as a 'curse' - it is who I am. Over the years, I have learned how to protect my personal environment and my energy. I make conscious decisions regarding who I choose to spend time with and what stimulus I allow into my environment. This includes TV, radio, newspapers, reading material, social media etc. I now choose not to watch the news. I found that when tragedy struck - as it often did - I would feel the pain of those involved. I began to notice the physiological changes in my body. My breathing became shallow, my pulse increased, and I began feeling anxious. When images of the little Syrian boy washed up on the beach were on every media platform available, I cried for weeks. So, I choose not to watch the news.

Researchers have established that the brain cannot tell the difference between fact and fiction because it is responding to vibration or energy. So, films, television shows (even advertisements) also affect me. I get caught up in the emotions of the characters. I feel what they feel - which is usually highly entertaining for my family when I am crying during a film, TV show or an advertisement. I also find being in crowds very overwhelming, as there are so many energies and emotions in a confined space. So, as you can imagine, Christmas shopping is certainly a challenge for me.

Over the years, I have developed a range of strategies that have helped me to function as an empath in a world that is, at times, overwhelming.

1. I protect my personal environment - I choose the stimulus I engage with to ensure that it is uplifting.
2. I meditate and release what does not belong to me.
3. I am mindful of who I spend my time with. I limit the time I spend with people who I find draining to be around or who are consistently negative.
4. I spend time alone. It does not need to be an extended period of time. Sometimes, this is simply when I am meditating, but it is important to be still and check in with myself.
5. When I am feeling a particular emotion, I check in and I ask myself whether or not it belongs to me. It can be tricky to determine this at first, but with practice, it becomes easier.
6. I spend time every day doing what brings me joy.

Being an empath is a gift that I use every day, often unconsciously now. I am the friend who seems to just know when to make the phone call, and I am inevitably at the right place at the right time. I work in education and come across a lot of students. I know when a student is struggling or when something has happened in their lives. This allows me to reach out and it also makes them feel like someone sees them - *really* sees them. Last year I had a Year 12 student who was struggling with anxiety and depression, but he was very good at concealing it. On the outside, he was a confident, carefree young man, but I saw through the facade - I felt the authentic truth. I remember asking him a simple question: "How are you?'. He said, "I am good, Miss". I smiled at him and said, 'No, you're not. I see you". With a wry smile he replied, 'I know'. In that moment he knew that I saw him and that I was there for him, and that was enough. At the end of the year, he gave me a card with only two words written inside - 'Thank you'. They were genuine and heartfelt, and meant the world to me.

My beautiful daughter is an empath too, and I feel so grateful that she chose me as her mother, so that I can help her to understand what she is feeling.

All children are empaths when they are very young. As infants they are keenly aware of, or in tune with, the energies in their environment.

However, unless nurtured, they lose the awareness of their connection and begin to believe that any emotion they feel belongs to them. Over time, they simply forget. I remember watching my newborn baby and how she studied others intently. Her response to others in her environment, based on the energy they were emanating was fascinating to watch. I vividly remember walking with her through our local shopping centre when she was three years old. There was a middle-aged man in our area who had experienced the trauma of losing his parents in a car accident when he was young. He was trapped in a moment and would carry a crumpled photograph in his hand, muttering to himself. He had good days, and days when he was visibly agitated. We would frequently see him as he walked through the centre. On one occasion, he was having a difficult day and was clearly agitated, yelling at people who walked past. My daughter looked up to me and said, "Mummy, that man needs a band aid". I asked her why and she replied, "because he has a sore heart". Her insight and compassion brought tears to my eyes, as it still does today, when I recollect this experience. It afforded me the opportunity to begin to speak to her about what she was feeling and that sometimes the feelings we have don't belong to us.

She is now nine, and will frequently say to me, "Mum, I've got that feeling again" when we walk past someone. She tends to pick up on a deep sadness or feelings of isolation within people. We then talk about the sadness she feels, so that she can learn to distinguish between what belongs to her and what doesn't. At times, this becomes too much for her and she has on a few occasions asked me how to 'turn it off'. I have explained that it is a gift and that it is one of the many things that people love about her. She has learned to meditate in order to help her process the emotions she feels when it becomes overwhelming.

Part of the meditation involves visualisation. She will picture the person involved and see a thin thread connecting the two of them. With the image clearly in her mind, she allows herself to feel the emotion and asks herself what it is that the person really needs. Invariably it is love in its many forms. She sends them love and watches the thin thread dissolve as she feels the sadness leave her body. By going through this small ritual, she is able to release what is not hers. Another technique we have used when she does not want to feel the emotion at all, is to imagine that she is inside a beautiful bubble of protective white light. In giving her these small tools, I have been able to teach her how to protect herself and value it as a precious gift. There are so many children out there who, like my daughter, feel things deeply but do not understand why. It is my hope that books like these will help to guide others to support our children as they navigate their connection.

I truly believe that everyone is an empath, but most people are simply not aware that they are - they have yet to tune in.

It is easy to understand why, given the many distractions there are in contemporary society. We are plugged in or connected to our devices 24/7 and spend very little time in silence, connecting to ourselves. For the most part, we do this unconsciously; we tell ourselves that we are just so busy and that the distractions are unavoidable. But, how many times have you heard someone say that they 'can't stand to be alone'? What is it about being alone, without TV, internet, or devices, that makes people so uncomfortable? Personally, I think that it is because it is only when these external distractions are removed, that we begin to tune in and hear the small voice that lies within. This small voice can be confronting, because it speaks truth. It is the path of least resistance, or the easy option to shut this voice out, to numb ourselves to all feelings, not just of those around us but our own.

Imagine a world where everyone was keenly aware of what they were feeling and how others around them felt. Confronting? Perhaps. But, I believe that it would lead to people stepping into their authentic self and developing a level of compassion for others rarely seen today. People would soon realise that they are *all* empaths, without exception. I believe that people would begin to recognise their greatness and seek to serve; to add value to all that they are blessed to encounter. Slow down, disconnect, breathe, check in, feel and recognise who you truly are. You are greatness! You are love! You are beautiful!

Michelle

Life as an Empath

Robin Pantours

"When life has brought me to my knees, I will still pull you to your feet."

I was born into a military family, a revolving door of endless moves to various parts of the Australian coast and south East Asian locations. From a young age, it was assumed my strong-minded nature was enough to stand alone, while the softer nature of my eldest sister required a mother's protection and support. My childhood was just that; left alone with my imagination and instinct to carve out connections with people who I would only know for a few years before moving again.

It came naturally to me to read groups of people and adapt, and to immerse myself in the existence of their world. From such a young age, I sought to belong, while never feeling I did. It wasn't just about belonging. For this feeling to be appeased, I required to understand, I observed, I listened, and I felt with such intensity that more often than not, a deep sadness lay bare on my child-like heart. In those early years, I sought solitude in writing and drowning myself in books that expanded on my quest to understand the human condition and distracted myself from the loneliness I so often felt.

In the beginning of my teen years, I found myself living with my family in South East Asia. By this time in my life, the need to feel a part of something grew with such intensity that I felt I couldn't get enough air in my lungs to sustain the emotions I felt. It was at this time that my family emotionally stepped out of my life, and things began to get complicated. In those early years, I explored foreign countries with my much older punk rock Muslim boyfriend who happened to have a raging drug addiction, and it seemed only natural for me to go along for the ride in search of connection. I turned my back on the western world, dropped out of international high school and spent my days studying Islam, using drugs and travelling Asia. My need to connect and understand was so much so, that the English language became my second preference as my speaking tongue. When you are given the gift of feeling and knowing at such a young age, it can feel more like drowning than as a tool for the greater good. I was self-destructive in nature, turning my back on the intensity of my feelings, and I developed a preference for numbing through drugs and sex.

By the time I was sixteen, I had a drug addiction, I had been sexually assaulted, and my family was broken by my father's ongoing infidelity (which I was threated to keep my mouth shut upon the discovery of pornographic images of my father's conquests). My mother, with my sister under her wing, returned to Australia to look after my dying grandmother. The Christmas before I was to return to Australia, I spent alone overdosing on my family's bathroom floor with no one to rescue me. I returned to the Land of Oz not long after that, with every intention of going back to Asia to marry and live my life in accordance with the law of Islam. But, it was not long before I found love in a self-destructive teenage boy with a beautiful musical gift and thought maybe, he was home. Like most young love, it was heightened, passionate, destructive and complicated. I was drowning in my grief and dysfunction, and with the forced decision by adults to terminate a wanted pregnancy, the normality and belonging I craved slipped away from me.

At seventeen, my mother moved out of the family home I was sharing with her and my sister and went off to marry the first man she met in a secret wedding hidden from the family unit. She put my sister and I in a little apartment and went on her way, to endure a controlling and violent man that laid hands and bitter words on me for years to come, resulting in my mother using a napkin placed under my door, telling me she could no longer be my mother. This push and pull remained in my life for years to follow. My father moved to Dubai with his new foreign wife, but would often call me, suicidal, after he was discovered to be having yet another affair. These suicidal phone calls after an affair became a normality in our father-daughter relationship.

In a bid to find this feeling of love of connection and to escape that all too familiar feeling of sadness, I moved onto another relationship. *This time, I would make it work. This time I would belong to a family; my own family.* I spent the next ten years trying to build a life with someone who tore me down at every chance he could. A man that inflicted such wounds on my already fragile heart, that to this day, the scars remain a silent reminder of my perceived failings at creating a life I longed for. But all I saw was his inner pain, and thought that with enough love, he would love me back. If I was perfect enough and remained still enough in my passionate and determined nature, he would see how special I was. We brought two sons into the world on the back of my broken heart and shattered dreams. As a mother, I felt the weight of the world in trying to raise these boys and ensure no pain became theirs, so much so, that I developed anxiety and depression that would follow me for years to come, along with an ingrained belief that I was not worthy of love.

At twenty-eight, I became a single mum and attracted every narcissist person under the sun. *Surely, I could bring light to their heart, for after all, I understood them and their broken selves.* At this stage in my life, I had been working in the welfare sector for eight years, and my passion for my work was led by my ability to read between the lines of people's stories. I felt humility in their journey and sought to alleviate their pain and sufferance, even at the cost of my own wellbeing. I held babies born to neglect and trauma, I offered hope to people in great pain, and I took every story as a personal goal to bring something positive to their existence, in the hope that they could heal.

In my thirties, I went on to marry a kind man; a man that made me feel that he could handle my emotionally heavy heart, and my hope was that I would find solace in his loving arms. During this marriage, my third son was born, but not before a hospitalisation for panic disorder and the ongoing guidance of a peri-natal psychiatrist. After years of running and years of hurting and feeling, so began my undoing, and the undoing of our marriage.

It was in my journey to my knees that I now understand that I never allowed myself to walk first.

I assumed that I was enough if I was helping others, and I that was strong enough to not need help myself. I was unware that I was reaching my capacity; that my anxiety was tearing me apart and building walls in places that should have been open spaces.

I left the welfare industry and went on to study mind and body healing and opened my own holistic therapy business. My passion for conversation and healing was a driving force. The ability to build connections and bring light to people was such a privilege and honour. It never felt like work; it felt like living.

Then, came the darkness. A darkness that my life journey had only ever dipped its toes in. My little boy - my second born - attempted to take his own life at the tender age of seven. His deep sense of unease for this world lead him to think that this life was no place for his vastly expressive mind and determined spirit. A mother's connection to her child is so fierce, and of course, I would not rest until I knew I could save him. As a mother who is an empath, there are no words great enough to fit the enormity of my heart tearing apart in my quest to shine light on my son. But, I was soon to understand that the universe would further bring me to my knees. This little boy, my child, my son, was not long afterwards diagnosed with leukemia, and now I am to walk beside him, watching his body fight this horrible and unfair illness. The image of this first breath as he was placed into my arms over seven years ago remains etched into my mind, as I hold him through the pain of chemotherapy and endless hospital visits. And it is in this moment, that I understand my undoing. My often-endless empathic cup is not just overfilling; its smashed into shattered pieces on the cold reality of the ground. My once natural ability to just 'feel' is choked in a clasp of pain that grips like weighted anchors to my feet, dragging me under the waves of the ocean.

It is now that I understand the life of an empath. I spent years feeling every emotion with such depth and allowing people to place these experiences in my path, so I could turn them into an energetically focused transaction to heal others. I defined my worth on my ability to give myself in mind and body to anyone who reached for me. In doing so, I assumed that I was living my higher purpose and I was doing the work I was born to do. But, it has come at such a great cost to my inner essence, my spirit, and my relationships. My son's struggle has brought great reflection on the need to allow myself time to tap into my own existence, step away and heal from the years on running and searching. I can't bring myself light if I am using all my matches to light the candles of others. This is not me saying I don't care; this is me saying that I have to care more about me, to be able to continue walking in this world.

So, in the midst of the greatest storm that has passed over my spirit, I have decided to wrap my empath up. For so long, I have laid bare, absorbing the pain of others, and now I have come to a place where I am required to turn down the sad songs, turn off the tragic news stories, turn away from people who for so long have required the part of me that takes the most from me. I am emerging, cutting the ropes one by one from the anchors that have kept me under the ocean's waves, and swimming upwards to the break of daylight above the surface.

I am allowing myself to breathe for the first time in my life.

In light of my son's diagnosis, I have been surrounded by my community's love, assistance and support. I had searched for so long to feel a part of something, not even realising that through living my truth and being a light to others in time of need, I had created a tribe of giving and loving souls who have now reached out for me. As an empath who by nature is introverted and often drained by social interactions, I have been challenged to let others give light to me. I have come to understand that I am loved and am truly humbled by this. I am taking breaks from the world, putting my feet in the ocean more, sitting under the strength of tall trees, and surrounding myself with people who not only allow me to lay down, but will lay next to me as I figure this out. When I came to the decision to step back and sit with my broken cup, I became more aware that this cup has served me well but can no longer be the cup I take breath from and give myself from.

In the solitude of deep reflection and great heartache, I am more aware that to give to others, I must stand from a place of inner love, and battle to find stillness in my restless mind and shattered spirit. I am to rise above my own demons and come to an acceptance of allowing peace to find me, as I don't have to feel *everything* to be guided in my journey of healing others. "What's mine is mine, and what's yours is yours", and I will stumble to be okay with this.

As an empath, I have walked around with the accumulation of others' karma, emotions and energy, and to me, this is but a gift and a curse. I am a listener of life and a keeper of light. For now, I choose to rest. I choose to allow myself the space required to love myself and in turn, grow in my capacity to heal others without comprising my own sanity. 'When life brings me to my knees, I will still pull you to your feet', but this time, I will make sure my knees don't remain on the ground too long, and I will drink from my own cup before filling others. With each exchange of energy presented before me, I will ensure that this energy will not always sit within, but rather wash over me as I release and surrender the higher purpose of the universe, in knowledge that beautiful things grow from adversity. I will listen, and I will feel. Empathy is a choice, and has been one that connects with my vulnerability, as in order to connect with people, I have had to connect with something within myself that knows that feeling.

I am grateful for the journey and honoured to contribute to a greater good. For the first time in my life, I can speak my truth and value my sensitive side I can show myself the same compassion that I'm so quick to show others. In protecting my inner empath, I am healing myself, and this can only benefit my work and life on the rest of my journey. With peace in my heart, I choose to heal.

Robin

My Personal Journey as an Empath

Ros Sharp

I believe I was born an Empath. I do not believe you can aspire to be an Empath, but rather it is something you are gifted with at birth. I believe most, if not all Empaths are born healers.

God delivers us this gift to share with the world - having a heightened sensitivity to the world and everything within it. An Empath has the ability to feel not only their own energy, but that of others, and is also relevant to emotions and feelings, for example pain, distress, feelings of sadness/happiness etc. They have a deep sense of feeling for others, to the point where they sometimes struggle to differentiate if what they are feeling is their own or that of someone else.

For me, being an Empath was unfortunately discovered in the latter part of my life (approximately about four-five years ago), and had I had the opportunity of finding this out when I was much younger, it would have made my life very different, a lot more manageable and with less confusion. A lot less self-doubt, I suspect. In saying that however, I do not look back on this with regret, because I have learned some pretty hard lessons along the way that have allowed my soul to grow exponentially during my lifetime, and I don't believe I would be the person I am today without having learned these lessons. I truly believe everything happens for a reason, and genuinely the way it is meant to, for each individual. "What doesn't kill us, makes us stronger," springs to mind here.

Strangely enough, it was through a friend who had shared an article with me on Facebook requesting me to read it, as she herself being an Empath, believed I too, was one. She could see through my posts at the time that I was somewhat struggling with things. It was an article on "The traits of an Empath".

After pouring myself into this article, I discovered I ticked every box in the check list and my life all of a sudden made a lot of sense. Following reading this article, I indulged myself in as many articles as possible on being an Empath to further educate myself on the topic, as I contemplated why it had taken me the best part of my life for this to reveal itself to me. I felt like a veil had been lifted and a whole new world was opening up to me.

Right from a very early age, I always knew I was somewhat different to my peers, but growing up as a child, I never knew why I was different. I felt isolated, shy and had trouble mixing with other children. I had a feeling of being constantly overwhelmed by the world and everything within it.

I lacked confidence and would keep to myself, not really knowing how to mingle with other children. I felt like I lived in my own little bubble and at times felt quite ostracised.

From birth, I have always been a hyper-sensitive person, which can oftentimes be affiliated with being an empath, but this isn't always the case. For me, I have an extreme sensitivity to bright light, sound/noise, energy, food additives and chemically laden processed foods among others. I have since learned that this, these days is labelled as a Highly Sensitive Person (HSP).

"A highly sensitive person is known to have sensory processing sensitivity. A personality trait which defines a highly sensitive person has been described as having a hypersensitivity to external stimuli, a greater depth of cognitive processing and high emotional reactivity. " (Authors: Elaine Aron · Elaine N. Aron)

My experience as an Empath, as most empaths would agree, has been both good and bad. As you will hear, many empaths declare it can be both a blessing and a curse, but I do believe it to be a gift. It is vital for us as empaths to find ways to overcome the many things we struggle with on a daily basis and utilise this gift to live our true life's purpose. To heal the world, ourselves and others, we must find ways to get back to love and peace and be able to find calm among the chaos. The anxiety that builds within us is extreme at times, and we must learn to nurture ourselves, set boundaries and stay true and authentic to who we are as individuals. This is a gift that deserves to be nurtured, as does our soul.

Some of the many things I struggle with as an Empath are as follows:

I don't do well in crowds/public places -due to the intensity of everyone's energy. Because of this, I have a tendency at times to say no to invitations - preferring to stay at home and be in my own comfortable space. This can cause me to be somewhat of a hermit, which I have to keep in check, because it can get out of hand if I'm not mindful. Too much of this is simply not healthy (at least in my opinion).

I struggle at times, to differentiate between my own energy and that of others.

I constantly feel fatigued for all that I absorb throughout my day.

I struggle with anxiety at a high level, can get stressed quite easily and at times, feel so overwhelmed that I feel the energy within me is chaotic.

I have a constant need for solitude (to recharge, re-energise, rest & recoup).

I have a tendency to overeat - I believe myself to be an emotional and stress eater, which in turn has me overweight.

I abhor any form of cruelty to animals or any living creature.

I have an intolerance to bullying, any aggression toward others, violence in all forms albeit verbal, physical, emotional abuse and/or narcissism, hatred, racism and bigotry.

I cannot view photos or images of animal cruelty or view any violent pictures or films.

I have an extreme sensitivity to light (as mentioned above) but most especially to bright lights, flashing lights, fluorescent lighting and direct sunlight/glare. I also struggle with night driving due to the lights of the oncoming traffic.

I have an extreme sensitivity to sound (as mentioned above) be it loud noises, sirens, whistles, high pitched noises and almost zero tolerance to children screaming.

I feel the energy of everything and everything is energy, so I often feel chaotic due to for example, the energy of storms, lightening, of driving in heavy traffic, the energy of the Universe when it is crazy, of people arguing around me, of visiting a busy public place such as a busy shopping centre.

I struggle to speak on my mobile phone without utilising the speaker option, as the energy emitted from my phone whilst holding it to my ear is too much for me to handle.

Feeling the emotions and pain of other people. As an Empath, you not only get to experience another person's joy, but you also experience their pain and distress, which can overwhelm you at times. All you want to do is help/heal people and be able to take away their pain.

Some of the things I relish in being an Empath are as follows:

I feel the energy of a room before I walk into it.

No-one could ever creep up on me, as I would feel their energy first and know they were there.

I have an innate knowing when a person is being dishonest.

If someone is telling me they're okay, I will know it if they are not, or if they are trying to hide something.

I can easily relate to others and have a great understanding, compassion and empathy for others.

I am a good listener and people can automatically sense that what they confide in me, stays with me.

I can read people very well and will genuinely get a vibe from you the very first time I meet you, be it good or bad. I will feel your energy long before I get introduced to you or shake your hand.

I have an extremely strong intuition and consider myself also to be clairsentient to a degree.

I will always look out for the underdog.

People, sometimes ones I've just met, have a tendency to seek me out and tell me their problems. They look to me for advice, counsel, or to simply get my opinion or perspective on things.

I'm sure all fellow Empaths can appreciate, that having this innate gift can cause a lot of anxiety within the body and for me also at times, I've struggled with depression.

Following the birth of my only child - my daughter - at the age of thirty-seven, and the consequential breakdown of the relationship with her father just three months following the birth, I also suffered post-natal depression. Unfortunately, this then led me down the path of becoming reliant upon anti-depressants for the next nine years, purely just to function. Looking back now, having been off them for the past five years, I wish I'd have made the choice to get off them sooner.

Being on anti-depressants numbed me to the world and obviously stifled this gift of being an Empath during this time. I guess the only thing working in my favour at the time was the fact that I was totally oblivious to the fact I was an Empath, and only found this out at the age of forty-five. I am now fifty years old. Don't get me wrong, I believe anti-depressants have their place and help a lot of people, but I also believe doctors are all too happy to keep people on them far longer than is necessary at times, just to keep the pharmaceuticals and doctors' wallets lined. But, that's a whole other story.

What I discovered, coming off antidepressants was that my emotions were re-awakened. For the previous nine years, my emotions were simply flat-lined. I didn't really know when I was happy or when I was sad. I just simply felt okay each day and kept putting one foot in front of the other, as I busily raised my daughter single-handedly and did whatever I had to do.

Today, it's like I'm a very different human being. I feel emotions so strongly that I absolutely wear my heart on my sleeve. I could not hide my emotions from anyone for the life of me. What you see is what you get with me, and these days I am an extremely emotional being. If I'm watching a movie, even if it's simply a sad scene out of Home and Away, you will find me crying on the couch. As I'm watching it, I feel it is happening to me, and I feel their pain or sadness, whatever the case may be. I also experience tears of joy. Certain songs resonate within me and bring me to tears. I feel my emotional state is partly due to the fact that this side of me was stifled for nine long years. However, I never apologise for showing my emotions, nor do I feel weak, because unlike some people, I believe showing your emotions is a sign of strength, not weakness. It is a sign of strength to be able to show your most vulnerable side, and I know and understand many people who have different views on this. I also know people who don't like showing their vulnerable side. I am simply stating my experience and expressing my opinion upon it. Everyone is a unique individual and has their own life's experience, views & opinions upon this and I totally respect that.

Empaths often feel different to everyone else because of their sensitivities and all that they feel and experience on a daily basis. It is an absolute overload of the senses that does take its toll upon the body. We often feel like the odd one out, for people who don't have such sensitivities have difficulty in understanding those that do. For me, it's been especially hard in the workplace, trying to work in an office with many other ladies, all under fluorescent lighting when I have such a sensitivity to it. It's hard to please everyone because obviously you need light to see and sit at a computer, however even my computer screen has to be turned right down. It can cause even the slightest difficulties and make you feel somewhat odd when you have to speak with management to accommodate sitting in a position so as not to have the bright fluorescent lighting affect you or your work. This lighting causes me great headaches, and makes my eyes water and very red. Even walking into a shopping centre has this effect on me because of all the lighting.

Empaths can feel overwhelmed by the constant, ever present stimulation of day to day life.

Being an Empath is an absolute journey; one I regularly compare to that of a rollercoaster ride. It can be both joyous and happy, and also leave you feeling extremely anxious, drained and overwhelmed. As Empaths, we must remember why we are here and why we were the chosen ones to receive such a gift. Because of this, it is vital we stay true to our divine purpose and find ways to deal with the downside of being an Empath. By this, I mean it is a constant work in progress, but absolutely vital we find ways to protect ourselves, to forge boundaries, to shield from harsh energies, to nurture our soul, and to educate ourselves in finding the tools to assist us with strengthening our coping mechanisms for the things we struggle with daily.

Prior to knowing I was an Empath, I wasn't aware of the need for setting boundaries with certain people, and this can leave you open to being taken advantage of. In the past, I often attracted people of lower vibrational energies - who saw me as their light - and believed that I could and would fix all of their problems. I can see how this occurred, because I have a natural tendency to want to help all people whenever and wherever I can, however I am not a qualified psychologist. I have also come across many people who have no respect for the boundaries I have in place, and I must confess I have cut such toxic people from my life for my own self-preservation. If you have enough self-respect, you will do whatever is necessary.

It is absolutely vital to have these boundaries with people, or your generosity and kindness will be abused and will generally deplete you of all your good energy, leaving you running on an empty tank.

It is at this time I'd like to touch upon a subject, and that is the **relationship between an empath and a narcissist/sociopath.** You see, this is the relationship I shared with the father of my child for five arduous years but had no knowing of it at the time. This is first and foremost where I learned to set my boundaries. Sadly though, it wasn't until after the breakdown of this relationship. I learned the lesson the hard way. "You teach people how to treat you" is a quote I very much like and have used several times (Dr Phil McGraw).

I can see why we were drawn to each other in the beginning. He had experienced a lot in his life and had many issues as a consequence of such. Me, being who I was, thought I could finally be the girl he would meet who would ease his pain and fix his problems, or at best coerce him into seeking help for healing in his life, so he could move forward. Keep in mind, I was not aware during this time that I was an Empath.

Unfortunately, this relationship was always destined for disaster from the get go. I quickly realised you cannot change another person. You can only change yourself and work upon yourself, and the way in which you interact with others. You can offer to help someone, but if they're not willing to meet you halfway or aren't ready to help themselves, your attempt is going to be futile. I fell in love with this man because of his wit and his innate ability to always make me laugh; something I loved to do. Now, looking back, I realise he was using his quick wit to mask the pain he was truly feeling underneath at a very deep level. He did not wish to reveal this true side of himself, nor do the hard work it would take to address his pain, bringing it to the surface to be healed and therefore giving him the ability to move on. Instead, he used drugs and alcohol to bury his pain, so he would feel numb to the world. Quite sad really, because underneath all of this, I could see the good in him, as empaths quite often do. We see the good in all.

Sadly, not having a true sense of who I was at the time, some of my experiences in my relationship with the father of my child consisted of the following:

Finding myself exposed to verbal, mental and emotional abuse (domestic violence)

He wanted absolute control of me and would do everything in his power to isolate me from family and friends (my support network).

He was a compulsive liar.

He would steal money from me out of my wallet, my coin collection, wherever he could.

He would drive my car intoxicated and under the influence of drugs with no care in the world.

He had a complete lack of empathy.

He loved belittling me in front of others as soon as he had an audience.

He was extremely jealous & controlling. I had to remove any previous boyfriends' gifts, cards, letters, etc. to be with him.

He was arrogant, rude and obnoxious at times.

He had a grandiose sense of entitlement.

He was extremely manipulative and showed absolutely no signs of remorse or sorrow; nor ever apologised for any wrongful behaviour. In fact, he was blameless in everything. Everything was always my fault. (I have since learned when people are completely blameless and never admit to being at fault, they do this to deflect things away from themselves, as they don't wish to look at this part of themselves to heal or change anything. They are pretty much in denial).

Whilst I know this doesn't portray a loving relationship, I do believe it was all one sided. I always made the choice to look for the good in him. Looking back now, it seems I was foolish. I had such low self-esteem and confidence, I didn't think I deserved any better at the time. Narcissists and sociopaths are extremely manipulative people. They play mind games to the point you believe everything they are saying is true, which makes you doubt yourself continuously. You kind of think you are going insane. They charm you and know how to play you to get what they want. Their sole purpose for being in any relationship is to get their needs met and they have no compassion for your needs/wants. They will remain in the relationship until they have sucked you dry, and only when you've hit rock bottom, can you see you've been played the whole time. They never really loved you in the first place.

In 2004 when I'd had enough, and following my daughters' birth, I found the strength to kick him to the curb. I would never have raised my daughter in that environment. She is my world and has always meant everything to me. Sadly, he'd taken all but my soul with him and left me with nothing. I no longer had any self-esteem, savings, friends, job, the list goes on. Thankfully though, my family have always been there standing by me. I couldn't have come out of this without them.

Then began my healing process, which I believe is still ongoing today, to a degree; thirteen years later. I believe I have come a very long way and have done a hell of a lot of work on myself to build myself back up again, and I have to say, I am bloody proud of the person I am today.

Obviously, he came into my life for a reason, and I learned so many lessons and have not one regret, because without this relationship, I would not have my one and only beautiful girl by my side. This relationship doesn't come without lifelong scars, though. I believe I have done a lot to heal things within me, but I am yet to enter another relationship and have now been single for the past thirteen years. I do hope one day to find the love I know that I deserve and will now most certainly be aware of what I *don't* wish to attract in a partner. I know I will be most cautious and not settle for anything less than I deserve. In the interim, I am happy in my own skin, living my life as a single person, continuously working on myself and sharing an amazing bond with my daughter.

I chose to mention this as part of my personal journey, because I believe the relationship between an empath and a narcissist can be quite common and may resonate with someone else reading my story. It is very easy to have your heart open and be in a place of wanting to help someone, and unfortunately at times, you open yourself up to manipulative, apathetic people who are just out for themselves and ultimately, suck you dry. It was a hard five years, - way harder than it needed to be, and way longer than it should have been. I most certainly should have listened to my intuition, as it was screaming to me that I was in a toxic and extremely unhealthy relationship, but I believed I stayed for as long as I did out of fear. I absolutely feared him in the end and felt like I was constantly walking on eggshells around him, waiting for the ticking time bomb to go off. And, more often than not, it did with his heavy drinking and drug use.

I am extremely proud of myself for getting out when I did - putting my daughter first like any parent would - and am so proud of the beautiful young lady she has grown up to be. She would have been a very different human being should I have chosen to stay in that toxic environment. The stress was just too much in the end. My health was suffering, and I needed to step up for my daughter. If I went down, she would have had nobody.

Obviously in the world we live in today, as an empath I have had to dig deep to find ways to protect myself; to deal with the exhaustion, my emotions and the energies that my body absorbs. On a daily basis, I have to ground, clear and shield my energy. I rest my body and have solitude as required, and I have had to set strong boundaries with some people.

Things I have learned as an empath:

To ground, clear and shield my energy on a daily basis for protection.

To set boundaries with people. We teach people how to treat us, by that which we accept and tolerate.

To speak up for myself and use my voice, even though I hate confrontation immensely, but I have enough self-respect to stay true to my authentic self, knowing my feelings matter too.

The more I speak up for myself, the better I feel, and the less illness gets stored in my body due to stifled emotions.

To not hide my emotions, but show them as a sign of strength, not weakness.

To respect myself enough to walk away from situations that make me feel uncomfortable.

To take heed of my gut feelings/intuition, as it never proves me wrong.

To be aware of the vibrational energy I feel from a person when I first meet them, as this first impression is usually right.

That I am stronger than I believed possible.

That my soul has grown exponentially.

To accept my anxiety as part of me. I have also learned to breathe through it, and that it won't last forever.

The art of meditation as a way to focus and quiet the mind; restoring peace and calm back into my being.

To nurture myself and take power naps when I need them, to recharge, restore and re-energise.

That I like my alone time and my own space, which is vital for an empath to recharge, restore and re-energise.

To say no to invitations that invite me to places/situations I know I won't be comfortable in, due to the extremity of noise, crowds, lights etc.

To listen to the beat of my own drum and be in tune with myself and do only that which makes me feel comfortable and happy.

That when you give to yourself first, you have more to give others. This is an extremely hard lesson to learn as a mother, because the vast majority of us are completely selfless, and have always given to our families and children first. It's very important to keep your glass full, so you have more to give others.

For myself as an empath, it is a constant work in progress to find a healthy balance between alone time and becoming a hermit. I am naturally a home body and very comfortable in this space, but if I'm not mindful, it could potentially cause me to become a recluse or hermit and shut myself away from the world. I constantly have to remind myself to get outside of my comfort zone and step into the real world.

Some examples of how my soul has grown from childhood into adulthood are as follows:

In childhood, I was extremely shy and introverted and never spoke up for myself. I would keep my feelings shelved & stifled. As an adult, I have learned to speak up for myself, speak my truth and voice my opinions without fearing judgement from others.

As a child, I was bullied because people just didn't understand me, so they teased me. As an adult, I speak up and believe people respect me more for it. I don't let anyone put anything over me or dominate me.

As a child, I had no confidence or self-esteem. As an adult I do, but there is always room for improvement here.

As a child, I worried about what other people thought of me. This was instilled in us by our parents who grew up in an era where this really mattered. As an adult, I've reached an age where I steer my own ship. I no longer care about what other people think, because I know who I am to my absolute core and am happy in who I am as a person.

As a child, I hated being on my own. As an adult, I relish my alone time, which gives me the freedom to do the things I love and utilise this time to nurture my soul.

Some of the tools I use in everyday life to help me live my life as an Empath are as follows:

GROUNDING -A process that enables you to connect with earth energies via your root chakra (found at the base of your spine}, enabling you to balance both your physical body with your spiritual body. Stand in bare feet on the earth and allow the energy of the earth to rise up through the soles of your feet. You can also ground yourself by closing your eyes and envisioning trunks/branches coming out through the soles of your feet, expanding, growing and pushing deep down until they anchor down into the earths' crust. Or, by simply eating root vegetables that grow in the ground for example, potatoes, carrots, radishes, turnips, etc.

CUTTING ENERGETIC CORDS - Call upon Archangel Michael to come with his blue sword of light to cut though any negative cords or attachments that may have plugged into you in your past or present and remove all that no longer serves you for your highest and best good. Affirm: "May these now be cut and converted back into love".

CLEARING & CLEANING – Again, ask Archangel Michael to clean and clear all cells and systems within your body, using his pure divine white light to sweep away any sludge or anything that no longer serves you for your highest good,

SHIELDING - Request Archangel Michael to shield your aura and auric fields against any negative energies, entities, sources, negative self-talk, thoughts, doubts, insecurities and fears, and be shielded against all else but love, light and peace, allowing you to be at the highest vibrational energy possible, and loving in all interactions inwardly/outwardly.

Obviously, you can make these your own and choose to say something personal to yourself. This is just along the lines of what I request from Archangel Michael who is infinite and there to serve everybody who calls upon him.

MEDITATION- I also choose to meditate when I'm feeling chaotic or anxious, and whilst I personally struggle with quiet meditation, I find it very easy to focus with guided meditation, and anything that can quiet the mind has got to be good for the soul.

BUBBLE- At times, when I'm away from my comfort zone and feel intensity around me - be it in the workplace or wherever - I choose to take myself off to a quiet place, even if it's just for a few minutes, and put myself in a bubble. Call upon your angels for protection and envision yourself in a pure white, divine light filled bubble. This will shield you from harsh energies.

Bringing this now to an end, if I have helped at least one person with sharing my personal journey as an empath and the tools I use to personally help me on my journey, then my job here is done. But, do ponder this. Being an empath is hard work and when the energy of the world is often chaotic, remember to be your own best friend. The longest relationship you will ever have is the one with yourself, so remember to be kind to yourself and learn to love all the parts of yourself that make you, uniquely you. There is no one else like you in the world, so be the best version of yourself that you can be and keep on shining. Your role here on earth is paramount to our future little humans that we are raising, and what we do as empaths matters.

Roy

Transparency

Sharon Miralles

As an empath, I feel what others feel - their thoughts, feelings, emotions, fears - psychically from their subtle energy field. I feel their soul as if it lays bare for me to see with my spiritual senses. I feel others' pure energy of spirit, as well as their human energy with all its flaws, weaknesses, vulnerabilities and intentions as if they are completely open. I am at One with them. As an empath, I am also telepathic and know things without knowing how I know them.

The beauty and grace of being an empath is a gift which I embrace wholeheartedly in this path of service. It is an extraordinary path to walk and as life unfolds and my empathic abilities only strengthen and develop further - although at times challenging - I would not change it for the world. I know that as we evolve spiritually, so too do our empathic abilities, which are natural and God-given for a special purpose. All of us are unique, special and connected, whether we are aware of it or not. As an empath, we can feel this interconnection – this Oneness with others. This is where the beauty lies. If we feel what others feel, we can be of better service. We would also never harm another soul.

I use my gift for healing. It is an honour to be bestowed with this gift of healing grace which has helped me transform the lives of many others. It has not been an easy path and if I can share with you some of my wisdom and what I have learned along the way, it may make your journey as an empath a little easier. This gift has much beauty, but it also has many challenges. Through learning to explore my gift of being an empath, I found many ways to cope with and adapt so I can be of better service to the world, while at the same time protecting my sensitive nature and my own energy from the harsh repercussions of this gift.

I am an energy healer, working in the energy fields of others, who sometimes have great illness, dis-ease and energy imbalances. Quite ironically, empaths tend to pick roles in life where they help others often exacerbating the symptoms of an empath. Being an empath has assisted me more effectively in the healing process of others, as I completely understand them and feel what they are going through. This was a little overwhelming for me in the beginning. When I first began the hands-on healing practice of Reiki, my empathic abilities developed on a deeper level and it was truly challenging. I had no idea what was happening to me. When I first began to place my hands upon people and began working in their aura field or subtle energy field, I became violently unwell. I would become nauseous, break out in hot and cold sweats and feel like I was going to pass out. There were times that after touching someone, or even someone else touching me to give me a healing, I would feel so unwell from absorbing the energies of others that I could not get out of bed for days with unexplained symptoms and chronic fatigue.

I could always feel when the energies, thoughts and feelings were not my own, as I did not feel right in my own energy.

Some of my spiritual teachers in the past always made me feel like I was doing something wrong, as I was always very sick when I touched another person either during the healing or afterwards. They told me I was taking on the energy of another, or not releasing them properly after the healing, which was wrong. I tried many different methods to prevent this from happening. In time, through my own inner guidance and wisdom and exploring energy, I discovered that in fact, I was not doing anything 'wrong'. This was a very natural ability for me and part of my healing abilities. I feel what another is feeling in my body, so I understand the issue: what the symptoms are, the root cause of the illness, disease, discomfort or blockage and how the person can heal from it. I receive messages as to what they can do to change, reverse the symptoms and take part in their own healing process. When I understand this, then the discomfort I feel in my body dissipates. I have to feel this in order to assist them in the healing process. I have learnt that I must take on another's energy to effectively help them heal, so I have a deeper understanding of the problem and how I can best help them. Being an empath helps me to be a more effective healer. When I walk away from them, I can release their energy and not carry it with me.

As an energy healer, I learnt to only apply my empathic abilities during a healing or reading session in order to best help another. I have learnt to only feel what I need to feel in order to help them and not take on all of their energy. I do this by asking my Angels and Guides beforehand and through prayer. I ask to be a clear channel for the Creator's healing to flow and how I can be of service and best help another. I trust that what is most relevant to the healing at the time will be revealed to me. No more, no less. It is simple and Divine.

I only use my empathic abilities on those who seek my assistance through a reading or healing. Otherwise, I think if I were walking around in life and passing through the aura fields of others, I would not be able to cope. At times, I feel so overwhelmed being around large groups of people or in public places and often feel unwell after for days or weeks at a time. I find that my sensitivities are increasing as I evolve and become even more empathic. If I am feeling a bit low in my energy, I ask Archangel Michael to be with me and protect me from absorbing any energies that are not of the purest love. Once again, quite ironically, I do not believe in protection and only ask for this when my light is not as strong and vibrant as it should be, or if I am feeling sick or down; either emotionally or mentally.

I feel that the need for protection stems from fear.

I believe we are all One; connected and we should love one another. If we love, we should not fear. Anything either stems from love or fear, so I live from a place of love. Protection creates separation. If I protect myself, I am creating disconnection and fear of what I will 'pick up' from others. Instead, I remain open and fill myself with light and love. Through this process, as light and love expand from within me, negative energy is not drawn to me as like attracts like. I always aim to have my light vibrant and powerful - as it should be - as this way, only love permeates to and from my energy field.

I understand and acknowledge that others may feel the need to protect themselves. If one is not ready, not living in their pure light, not loving others and themselves, feeling fearful in any way, or for any other reason which makes them feel the need to be protected, then protection may be needed for a time. It is important to feel comfortable with whatever you do. Empaths will know what is right for them.

I also try to block my telepathic abilities to those who seek my assistance. In the world of spirit, we communicate telepathically, but there is still a certain level of mutual respect and privacy. On a human level, it is very easy for me to read people's thoughts and at times it is hard to block what comes very natural to me. I believe people have the right to keep their thoughts and feelings private and I do not like to use my abilities for curiosity. I feel this would be breaking the law of free will. I know I do not like it when others try to permeate my energy field without my permission for their own curiosity or agendas and I always feel when this happens and the motivations behind it. The only times I use my telepathic gifts for personal use is when I first meet someone, to see if I resonate with their energy: if they are a kind and trustworthy person and to tell if someone is lying to me. I ALWAYS know when someone is lying to me. This can be very hurtful, especially when it is someone close to me. This is a challenge I have struggled with greatly. However hurtful and disappointing it is to me, I just have to know that the person who has lied is, in essence, hurting their own soul and I cannot control their actions. This is on their own conscience.

As a sensitive soul, it is quite often a lonely journey. I prefer my own company and solitude and love simplicity and to be outdoors in nature. As an empath, it is very easy to become introverted and withdrawn from social life, understandably so. It is hard to find others who truly understand me. I find it is important to surround myself with my loving family and pets, and people who only wish the best for me. My home is my sanctuary and I imbue every corner with love. It is my retreat from the world. It is here that I recharge and replenish my energy when I feel depleted from the effects of life as an empath. Time alone is really important to do this. For me, the assistance from the Angelic Realm, my connection with my Higher Self and God and my practice of self-healing and meditation have been instrumental in my ability to cope with the reverberation to my sensitive soul from being an empath.

You, the reader may be an empath. Most of us are more empathic and feeling in nature than we realise. Empathic abilities can take on many different forms and are sometimes very simple and subtle. One clear thread runs through all empaths: we are highly sensitive and that is perfectly fine. It is important for you to know you are perfect just as you are. You are enough just as you are. You do not need to be afraid, deny or ignore your gifts. Embrace them with love and fulfil your highest purpose. Your empathic gifts help you with earthly life. Your feeling nature is a way for your soul to guide you. What a beautiful gift it is to be in touch with your soul and true spiritual nature. Although it is hard to be so sensitive and empathic, it truly is all worth it!

I would like to leave you with a beautiful quote:

'The beauty you see in me is a reflection of you'
~ Rumi

I see the beauty in you. I see the light in you. Let us be a mirror and see our own beautiful reflection in each other. More importantly, let's feel it!

With love, light and unity,

Sharon

Learning to Thrive as an Empath

Sheryl A. Stradling

"Toughen up!" Mother said when I cried as Grandma's pet terrier jumped up on me. "I don't know why you're so afraid of everything." As a child, my parents criticised me for being shy, overly sensitive and fearful. They told me to not take things personally. I was an only child until I was ten and spent most of my time with Mother or playing alone. I was so open to experiencing emotions that I took on her anxiety and fears as my own. I was too scared to walk to the next block and play with other children. At my birthday party, I flinched when my aunt handed me a lighted match to light the candles on my cake. I hid under the table and cried when it was time to open my gifts. I learned that I was 'different', and it was not a positive description.

I am a physical, emotional and intuitive empath. I have a big heart and naturally attune to others emotionally. I easily internalise their joy and pain. I always want to help and am the proverbial good listener. I am still (even in my seventies) somewhat naive about people's intentions. I can allow myself to be taken advantage of because I care deeply about others and want to be of service. I have an innate sense of connection with the earth, animals and plants. I'm able to receive guidance through a loving energetic bond with my ancestors in spirit and attune to the future in dreams or waking visions. Alternatively, I easily attract energy vampires, prefer silence and solitude to social interaction and become exhausted from sensory overload.

I cherish my enhanced sensitivities, and I've learned to use them to better myself and help others. I value my depth of feeling and passion for life, however, I haven't always felt this way. I've struggled to understand why I felt like an outcast and was easily hurt. We empaths are much more than just highly sensitive people. We deeply feel the emotional states of others and easily take on their illness or well-being. People are drawn to us because they sense our innate compassion. We lack the filters others have to block sensory information, and we need time alone to recharge ourselves and rebalance our physical and emotional energy. Being an empath can be a mixed blessing.

In grade school, I didn't fit in. I preferred to sit on the bench at the edge of the playground with the teacher during recess. I was un-athletic and timid. I was often excused from physical education activities and was the last to be chosen for anyone's team. I was a good listener, however, a magnet for my troubled, introverted and unskilled classmates. I helped the girls learn how to thread their needles when we were taught to sew. I was elected the class secretary. My classmates came to me, shared their stories, asked for help with their homework and went away feeling better.

In high school, I overcame some of my introversion and learned coping techniques. Encouraged by my teachers, I became an outstanding student and used my innate intelligence and curiosity to learn. My parents would have preferred me to be socially adept and popular. They attempted to change me into a social extrovert and sent me to a myriad of lessons which included ballet, swimming and ballroom dance. I responded by withdrawing into myself and spending my time reading or exploring nature.

I taught myself to meditate and use self-hypnosis. I felt drawn to Eastern philosophy and spiritual practices. They helped me find serenity in our chaotic family, which now included my two younger siblings. My sister was born when I was ten and my brother was born two years later. Mother continued to struggle with anxiety as well as physical illness for the remainder of her life. Her problems were never discussed, but they overtook the family. I developed a codependent relationship with her as I became her daily helper.

Aside from the lessons my parents sent me to, I was rarely allowed to socialise outside of school. Dad usually said, "You might be needed at home". Mom's typical response to my requests to go out with friends was, "Maybe". When my chores were done, I slipped out the back door and walked through the neighbourhood alleyways alone, wiping my tears while I prayed for inner peace. I'd always loved plants and seeing the colourful yellow nasturtiums spilling over broken fences onto the gravel calmed me as I walked.

"Don't take your own temperature", Mother admonished me when I shared my hurt feelings about a quarrel with a girlfriend, "you're too self-involved". It was her way of telling me to keep my sensitive emotions to myself and not to be who I was; an empath. She protected her own feelings by burying them and covering them with sarcastic humour. Confused by her words and sensing something was wrong with me, I retreated further into myself.

I decided to quit feeling emotions. It sounded simple; a rational solution. I had no idea what damage that would cause me emotionally or how long it would take to undo.

Despite my resolve not to feel deeply, typical teenage emotional fluctuations sent me into a see-saw of extreme reactions. I also experienced the jagged emotional variations of my few good friends. Again, I was drawn to the sensitives - empaths and outsiders who often struggled with self-esteem, social isolation or dysfunctional family patterns. We found solace in each other's company and soothed one other's feelings the best we knew how.

The next two decades of college and marriage were equally difficult. The codependent pattern I'd developed with Mother followed me into marriage. There was also little heart-connected love and acceptance in my marriage. I perpetuated the patterns of my family by marrying a man who was emotionally unavailable. I was torn between conflicting emotions of love and anger when I felt a deep connection and was hurt in return. We eventually divorced, and I became a single parent with three young children. Once again, I put my emotions on ice while I struggled to support my family, take on dual roles of breadwinner and nurturer and help my children deal with divorce.

As my children matured and eventually left home to start their own families, I matured also. I recognised I needed help and went to therapy. I found healing in a loving group of women from similar dysfunctional backgrounds. I began journaling regularly, recording dreams, and sharing my feelings in the group. It was the first time I felt accepted for the deeply sensitive person I had tried to hide for years. Although still unfamiliar with the word 'empath', I finally recognised that my depth of emotion, ability to sense energy and receive guidance from spiritual realms were gifts I could embrace and use to help myself and others. I became a lay leader in our group and supported my new friends as we grew together.

After divorce, I explored new relationships with men. This was before I understood that I am a relationship empath. I easily absorb my partner's emotions and stress. For a long time, I intentionally chose not to live with my partners. Too much togetherness makes me anxious. It impinges on my need for personal space and quiet. I prefer living alone. It's difficult for me to set healthy emotional boundaries and share my needs. I often prefer to sleep alone, too, a trait that one of my partners found unacceptable. He accused me of sabotaging our relationship when I suggested it. I am also stressed by loud noises such as my partner watching TV while I'm reading. I now understand my extreme sensitivities. However, until recently, I did not know how to express my needs in a close relationship.

There is nothing more wonderful and fulfilling than heart-centered and loving sexual intimacy. I love being physically affectionate and intimate with a partner I feel close to. My sensitivities increase as I get to know my partner better and my feelings deepen. During intimacy, energies are shared. I easily pick up on my partner's stress, intuit his thoughts or feelings and can sense his physical sensations. There is no 'casual sex' for me. I have never been able to argue and make up afterward with physical intimacy. Once I've absorbed anger and stress, I need time alone to recover. For me to feel comfortable in a relationship, I need to share reciprocal love and respect for each other's needs.

I have often been single. I've had trouble understanding why I couldn't form happy and lasting intimate relationships. I tend to gravitate to potential partners who are unavailable either emotionally or physically. Due to my enhanced openness, I fear losing myself and my freedom in a relationship. It is hard for me to commit. One partner accused me of being a 'commitment-phobe'. He was correct. At the time, however, I didn't understand the dynamics of my conflicted feelings in intimate relationships. Instead, I felt isolated and thought something was wrong with me.

When I have connected in long-term relationships, my partners usually had different ideas than I did about what a relationship should look like. One traditional partner urged me to support his needs by following conventional male and female roles, embracing his extroverted lifestyle and having constant interaction. Being around him drained me from the day we met, but I didn't know why. Unable to articulate my needs or set appropriate boundaries, I fell into the pleaser trap. I couldn't be what he needed but I kept trying. Once I understood myself better, I gained the courage say "no", and ended the relationship.

Despite these challenges, the better I know myself, the more I appreciate being an empath. This has taken a lifetime of therapy as well as personal and spiritual growth. I've learned the importance of physical, emotional and spiritual self-care. I exercise, eat natural foods, and use herbs, essential oils and Epsom salt baths to relax and replenish myself.

Meditation, time alone and enjoyment of nature strengthen my spiritual connection to myself and God.

Although I am an empath, I have a Type A personality. I'm goal-driven, ambitious and competitive. It's easy for me to spin into anxiety, shallow breathing and needless worry. To counter this, I've learned Reiki, Chi Gong and deep relaxation techniques. I write in my journal often. This helps me release and understand my emotions. My spiritual practice includes daily meditation, prayer and quiet time to connect with Source. I'm an incurable nature-lover and enjoy gardening. Digging in the dirt heals my soul! I forget every worry when I am attuned to the plants in my garden.

We live in a world of escalating terror, war and natural disaster. It is difficult to escape the news because it is everywhere; on our devices, in shopping malls and at the pump when we fill our tanks. In addition, advertising reminds us of our desires, weaknesses and addictions. It stimulates our 'need' for products to make us happier, healthier and sexier. Empaths are especially sensitive to these stressors. We require special strategies for self-protection and calming. Awareness of how we absorb and use energy is vital to how we feel, cope and shield ourselves.

As empaths, we need to stay energetically focused in order to circumvent negative or scattered energies. Our individual energy fields are constantly assailed by a confusing array of forces in our environment. We deal with this assault at work, on public transportation and freeways, and in crowded shopping malls. We blend our energies with others so easily it often throws us off balance. We can suddenly feel depressed or even ill without realising why.

Knowing how to use energy is the key to keeping our own energies intact. As we become more conscious of the energetic patterns we both use and encounter, we can connect with others in more positive ways as well as guard ourselves.

I find it challenging to remain focused. A technique I use daily is to 'ground and surround'. I ground myself to the earth by imagining energy stretching down from my feet and the base of my spine deep into the earth and being tethered there securely. This stabilises and centres me as well as creating inner strength and confidence. I also imagine filling and surrounding myself with protective golden light. This provides an energetic barrier to negativity, hostility or psychic attack. It helps prevent me from taking on unwanted energies. When I drive or use public transportation, I imagine the vehicle, train or plane is safely surrounded by light or grounded to the earth.

I also guard myself in potentially confrontational situations by imagining a clear barrier between me and the other person. This creates energetic separation and helps prevent taking on their emotions. Another method I use is to imagine several differences between me and the other person. This creates rational separation. I tell myself something like this: I'm a brunette, she's a blonde. I have on slacks, she's wearing a skirt. I am tall, she is short. It doesn't matter what item or characteristic I choose. Just noting the differences rationally separates me from the other person and allows me to strengthen my own persona and energy field.

Deep breathing reduces tension. I often remind myself to breathe when I start to feel anxious or experience sensory overload. I also use the Heart Math Institute's 'quick coherence technique' of breathing slowly and deeply through the heart and chest area while creating a positive feeling. This helps to reduce stress and induce a calm focus. For more information, see their website, www.heartmath.org.

When we breathe consciously and relax, we become more mindful. Mindfulness is the ultimate empath experience. It is the ability to be totally present in each moment while being aware of emotions and physical sensations. Meditation, yoga, Chi Gong, breathwork and other energy management techniques foster our ability to be mindful. Mindfulness allows us to create a calm focus which gives us greater choice and awareness. As a practice, it increases our ability to be serene.

I use affirmations and visualisation daily to create the life and feelings I want to experience. I deprogrammed much of my negative childhood upbringing this way. I affirm that what I desire in my life exists now, in the present. Faith and trust bolster me. Faith means believing in the reality of what has not yet appeared in physical form. Mind is the creator. Emotion is the power that boosts the creative process. When I say or write affirmations, I imagine how I would feel having that quality or item in my life now. I repeat simple affirmations silently (for example, 'Being an empath heals me.') before going to sleep or on awakening. The subconscious is most receptive at these times and will create what we affirm.

I tend to be a loner. I grew up alone and found it was the easiest way to protect my tender feelings. But we empaths need strong social support networks. This can be problematic because of our sensitivity. We need to find people like ourselves and create caring groups and relationships. I've honed my intuitive power to draw positive people and circumstances to me. I belong to several social groups based on common interests; writing, art, gardening and spiritual study. I make a point to give myself time to play, go on 'artist dates' and be adventurous. This provides self-soothing; it permits the space and time to nourish my intuitive and creative nature.

As I've learned to balance the energy I give to others with allowing myself to receive, I've become happier and more at peace. I've embraced flexibility and appreciate thinking outside the box. This is freedom. I can now claim my own space when I'm with a partner, sleep alone sometimes and have my own bathroom for the privacy I crave. I accept my needs and honour them. I am also learning the art of being emotionally neutral when necessary. Non-attachment can be a loving resolution. I can send others love and wish them well on their paths. It's a gift to trust others to solve their own problems. It is also a gift to ourselves. When we let go and let God, we reduce our stress and foster our own inner peace.

My life as an empath has been a challenging and healing journey. I'm a work in progress. I now appreciate my sensitivity and intuitive insight. I'm learning to allow my life to follow a winding, circuitous path of emotional experience and self-acceptance. It is the best way. It *is* the way. Some steps backward are okay and part of the journey. When I allow the path to unfold, I move forward ever faster.

I am still learning to share my needs. I honour my sensitivities with proactive self-care. I value my richness of emotion; it enhances my life. I am grateful for my intuitive ability to connect with spirit, heal myself and help people. I value being an empath and wouldn't change it for anything.

We empaths are kind-hearted and compassionate. We enjoy a deeply-felt connection with nature. We can amplify our intuition to spiritually guide ourselves and others. We possess the innate wisdom to change long-standing negative generational patterns. Our gift to the world is to experience deeply, feel deeply and help heal the world with the wisdom our sensitivities provide. We are bringers of light to a dark world of troubled souls. As empaths, we possess the vision and power to transform the planet.

Sheryl

My Journey as an Empath

Tracey Farrelly

– Tracey Farrelly, am going to share my story. Sit back and allow yourself to *feel* my journey as an Empath.

Walking into a shop with the intention of buying a new light – then suddenly feeling knots in my stomach and a lump in my throat, I wanted to cry. I felt intense sadness. This is just one of the times I knew I had to reach out to see if I could help someone. I asked the lady behind the counter if she didn't mind me asking, "I can feel your sadness - can I help?" Then this beautiful kind looking face asked, "How did you know"? I explained that I'm a psychic and an empath - I felt her pain. She shared with me that her mum had just passed away.

Being an empath is a gift, which is a blessing with both positive and negatives. It can physically make me sick, so it's vital for my wellbeing to protect myself spiritually.

Everything has energy, and an empath picks up this energy not only from other people, but spirits too (people who have passed over). Items such as furniture, clothing and jewellery also carry energy. I once held a piece of clothing not knowing whose it was and saw how someone passed over; it was not of their own choice, either. This was extremely traumatic for me and to this day, has left an imprint in my mind - feeling their fear, the sense of loss from their family, and how they just wanted to be laid to rest.

I know I've always had the gift of being an empath, although I have not always been in tune with it. I grew up in an abusive home. I just 'knew' when to be quiet, hoping the anger and abuse would just float by me. It was painful because I could feel it in the pit of my stomach; I knew what was coming next. On the flip side, knowing how genuinely happy other's lives were and being able to be a part of that, and feeling the love of relatives and friends has left imprints in my heart forever. These were truly felt as a deep positive energy, which came with a sense of peace.

Empaths must find a way of releasing or not owning the feelings and energy they feel from others. I always protect myself with a personal affirmation and white light around myself from above my head, and then tied off under my feet.

Whether you realise you're an empath or not, you will usually be in a career of caring; e.g. nursing, teacher, doctor, caregiver or vet, just to name a few. You will find most volunteers are empaths, also. This is because they feel the urge to help others. It makes them feel good. I find that people instinctively know they can share their stories with you - happy or sad - and you'll empathise with them. It is a natural feeling for both sides. This isn't something that you can learn - you're an empath or you're not - naturally. Many don't really understand how it all works and can be critical or negative when you say you're an empath. That's okay; that's their journey or ego, and ego doesn't belong in this kind of world.

Being an empath, your life is affected daily by outside energies. Peoples' fears, happiness and moods can all be felt and impact your own energy. This is why it's so important to recognise that you are an empath and always protect yourself. Empaths can be extremely sensitive to outside influences, e.g. television or radio, as these bring with them subconsciously many varied feelings. Whether it's fact or fiction doesn't matter; they're still all being played out. Hence, they're able to be felt by an empath.

When I'm doing psychic readings, some clients when finished, want to then talk and release their feelings with regards to painful situations they've encountered. It gives them the feeling of releasing this energy and because I've protected myself, I can hear this and then let it go. It doesn't impact on myself or my life. I've often wondered and also been asked by clients, "Don't you worry about coming into contact with negative energy and it staying around you from others?" My answer is a definite *no*. I feel and trust that I'm attracting only clients with positive intentions. I've had to tell a couple of people over the years that I couldn't read for them, and the reason was I felt their energy was negative. So, to protect myself, I've refrained from being in their presence.

We've all heard of the term, "Go with your gut". Well, this is so true, and most people dismiss this. That's where people can follow the wrong path or engage with people who are not a positive energy for them. Most of the time, I feel when I'm talking with someone who sees the glass half empty or doesn't have the same 'good intent' as I do. I say most of the time because sometimes I've not listened to myself. This has later come out and left me with a very negative feeling or energy to have to deal with. I've then let it go, so I can release it.

Everyone feels empathy; some much stronger than others. Knowing where energy is from - yourself or from another - is sometimes hard to decide. For example, a client walks in and says she's had a horrible experience the last time she met with a psychic. What's the first feeling I get once I am near her? My stomach is in knots, my breathing is a lot faster and my chest is pounding. I know all of this isn't from my thoughts or energy, so I ask, "You must be a little nervous"? They say "Yes", and I spend a moment reassuring them. What brings me peace personally, is when another person has validated what I feel is exactly what they're feeling; whether it's with their own health issues, how someone passed, or an emotion they or a loved one is feeling.

Here are a couple of real examples of people's health issues - names etc. changed of course, to keep it all confidential.

I was seeing a darkish think wall with little circles floating around, then they merged with the wall. It started out small, then one became bigger and bigger. I then heard what sounded like a heartbeat, immediately followed by a feeling of extreme happiness. I had a sense of knowing that this was an embryo implanting in a womb and the start of a new life. The parents' excitement when they found out brought me to tears.

Visiting a hospital or nursing home can be quite emotional. Walking past a room in a nursing home a while ago, I sensed a shallow feeling in my stomach. It was like a hungry feeling, and I wasn't sure what it meant. I stopped, went back and looked through the open door to see a lady lying in bed, frail, seemingly asleep. I then saw a nurse and asked her, "Is that lady okay"? She said she's alone - not many family visit, and she's' quite frail." They didn't think she had much time left. She wasn't able to really eat, and she slept more than she was awake. I said a little prayer for her, knowing she was sleeping peacefully, as there was a slight smile on her face. I wondered what she was dreaming about, then heard a little voice say, "Swinging on the swings is so much fun". Obviously, a childhood memory.

Some helpful tips
Remember, everything around us - including ourselves - vibrates energy. Energy keeps vibrating whether it's from us or whether we're touching an object. It's important to

be aware of this. For example, someone may bring a piece of furniture into their home, let's say a secondhand lounge for their family. This comes with the previous owners' energy and those who came into contact with it prior to coming into your home. This is why I always advise people to cleanse things when they buy them second hand, e.g. light sage and move it around the item while its smoking or ring a bell and say a positive affirmation to clear the item of any negativity and fill it with love and happiness. The same goes for any car or home.

Being an empath, I suggest people also cleanse their businesses regularly; especially when purchased from someone else. This will give it a fresh energy and not allow any previous energies to remain. This way, it has a new, positive energy which will encourage happiness, health and abundance to come in.

Empaths need to save their own body and mind from taking on too much. You need to take care of yourself first, so you can then help others. Understand that you can't always help everyone, even though you may want to. If you feel overwhelmed, take a step back for self-preservation.

Most of the time empaths keep their feelings to themselves, as many don't understand what it means to be an empath.

Its' important to share your feelings with others when you know you can. This releases you from any pain or fear by holding it all in; even if it's a good feeling.

Empaths come in many walks of life; human and animal, young, middle aged and the older generation. Sometimes, it may take someone a lifetime to really recognise and realise what it is they're feeling and taking on is empathy.

I thought I'd share a little of what it means to be an empath and a psychic by sharing a few of my experiences with you. For privacy reasons, I have named them Client 1, 2 etc.

Client 1 Feeling a sense of panic, being frightened to move, then sharp intense pains in my side, over and over again, followed by what felt like a quick hit to the side of my head left me feeling confused as to what happened to this gorgeous blonde-haired lady in spirit who came into the reading with my client. She let me know she once walked very tall and carried herself with perfect posture. She also gave me a quick flash of being a nurturing mummy, then a feeling of intense sadness, knowing she wouldn't be able to be with her darling daughter in the physical world ever again. Shortly after these pains, I felt numb. My client validated that her mum was once a model and indeed had blonde hair and carried herself very elegantly. She was grabbed and stabbed in the side several times and then was hit on her head with a blunt object.

Client 2 Tears rolled down my clients face as I explained sensing someone had been dishonest with them; someone who should always have been truthful and honest with them. Then, I got the feeling that their relationship had 'lost its spark'. I was shown a couple together and the feeling of being in love in a new, exciting relationship. This was validated by my client that her husband had admitted to having an affair and over time, had fallen emotionally in love with the other woman. He had said he was leaving, but she was hoping he'd change his mind and stay. However, he'd fallen for this new life with his new love.

Client 3 I was holding a piece of material, not knowing where it came from or who it belonged to. Then, I was shown in detail how someone was sad, as they'd been arguing with their partner. I was shown what someone did to hide the fact that they had hurt someone. This was very intense and something I hope I never see again. I wonder what can make someone go so far as to hurt or kill someone. It's a scary world at times; especially when you are shown how easily someone can do the above, then move on with their life as if nothing happened; leaving behind carnage for others to have to cope with for the rest of their lives.

A range of clients When someone comes through in spirit and their loved one - whether it be husband, wife, daughter, son is sitting in front of me, it's very intense. They allow me to feel what they felt leading up to them passing over, and also what the person sitting opposite me feels right now. I'm left with such a feeling of emptiness and sadness when they mention their loved one sitting right here with me. When they allow me to feel their symptoms leading up to them passing over, my heart may race because they died from a heart attack. They may show me lights in front of me on a road, then a sudden stopping, which may mean they died in a car or bike accident on a dark road where only their headlights were shining, and they hit a tree or another car. They may let me hear a baby crying for only a brief period, then silence, and I just know it was a baby which only survived for a very short period after birth. They may make my stomach sore, then my throat sore, which may mean they had a form of cancer which made them sick or started in their stomach area and travelled to their throat area. They may give me the feeling that my throat is closed, which usually means they weren't able to speak in the end, leading up to them passing. They could point to my ears or give me a tingling in my ears which means they were able to hear what was said to them. All of the above is given to me for validation for the client to know their loved one is still around them. They then also know that the validation of what they felt was how they passed.

All of our senses are heightened as an empath. Below are some examples of this.

SMELL for example, comes up often. I may smell a rose, and this could be because someone was given one or someone had them in their garden, or someone in spirit is acknowledging that they were placed on their resting place.

SIGHT I may be shown a home and the layout of a home, which may have been someone's family home prior to them passing. I could be shown a plan for a home that a client may be building. They may not even be aware this is about to happen for them. Another common example is a P plate with a tick above it shown to me, which means the client has someone (if not themselves) who is about to get their P plates.

SOUND I may hear a church bell ringing, which could mean someone is about to be proposed to and get married. I could hear the ocean and see a boat on it; someone may be about to go on a cruise.

FEELING I may feel a fuzziness in my head from someone who has passed over which is either indicating to me that they were highly medicated, or they had Alzheimer's. I could feel a sense of urgency and that could mean the person is just in a hurry or they could be panicking about something about to happen. Nervousness is a common feeling that is misinterpreted. It could be a sensation in the stomach and not mean nerves, but that the person has an ulcer.

It's so important as an empath to put all the senses together to understand the entire picture. I've learnt through actions, that if I'm not sure what something means, I should just give this information to the person I'm talking to, and they will likely know immediately; if not, they will eventually know what it all means.

An empath isn't always consciously aware of who they are feeling empathy towards or who they're feeling it for. This can happen when in a crowded shopping centre or football stadium, for example. As there are so many people around, it can be overwhelming to a lot of people, but especially to an empath. If they're not aware of how to protect themselves prior to going into these situations, it can be too much for them to bear and they need to remove themselves.

The positive experiences are most definitely more than the negative ones. I know I've been given the ability to recognise this gift as an empath. I'm grateful to be able to share just a little of what my journey has been so far, and I look forward to having many more experiences in the future.

Eternally grateful,

Tracey

The Empath Mum

Christie Lyons

Being a Mum of three children who are empaths just like me has been interesting to say the least. I wouldn't change it for the world, though. This beautiful gift allows me to have regular insight into their wellbeing that is astoundingly accurate, which when managed effectively, makes my job as their Mum so much more rewarding.

If only I had this insight when I was a child. I was such a shy, sensitive little girl and little did I know back then that a lot of the reasoning behind this was because I was picking up on so much energy from those around me. My family regularly remind me of how every single time they had a party or some kind of large gathering, that I would suddenly become ill. Looking back now, it's not surprising to me at all. The wonderful thing about being aware of all of this as an adult is that I can now provide the support and guidance to my own children that I so clearly needed in my own childhood. I am blessed enough to be able to share knowledge and management techniques with my children, so that they can grow up as empowered and emotionally healthy individuals.

We all know that being an empath isn't always easy.

Nor is being a parent; but when you combine the two, it can be mayhem at times. Of course, being both a Mum and an empath has its rewards, too. You can probably imagine that in addition to the everyday challenges that being a parent entails, adding this gift to the mix certainly makes for an interesting experience day in, day out.

Don't get me wrong; being an empath as a mother gives me some wonderful advantages. Having this 'knowing' means that I'm able to relate to my children on such a unique level, and the majority of the time, I needn't even ask what's going on with them, because I just 'know'. Even if there's not necessarily anything amiss with one of my children, I still know exactly what they need at any given time; whether it means they're getting sick and need a cuddle or are feeling over-excited about something coming up.

For example, when my youngest son was two years old and not quite verbal yet, he could simply look at me and I'd know exactly what he needed or wanted without trying to figure it out by questioning him. Sometimes, I was even onto it before he was!

The difficult side to this gift is being able to feel my children's emotions as my own when it becomes overwhelming for me. As everyone does, we all have challenges in life to deal with, and emotions of our own to understand and process, but when you add three more little people's emotions to this, it can become quite daunting and make you feel like you're carrying around the weight of the world. For example, if my teenager is feeling all hormonal and confused about his world, I feel it too. If my baby girl feels heartbroken because she's had to wave goodbye to Dad for the day, I feel it too. You get the gist...

At times, I've felt like just curling up in a ball and crying, and that's okay, because it can be a very overwhelming gift to have. But at the same time, I am extremely blessed to be able to share this wonderfully deep connection with my children. Once I was aware of what it means to be an empath, and learnt more about it, things started to become much easier, and I now see this gift in a whole new light. I am no longer afraid of being an empath and I believe that this is the key to embracing it wholly and healthily.

Up until recently, I was an avid believer in the need for performing protection rituals, such as white light bubbles, prayers, calling upon archangels, and the like; practicing them regularly to make sure I was safe at all times, and to help me feel as though I was protected. I still do teach some of these rituals to my children (and others), as it provides them with a visual and helps to give them a tool to use in order to help manage this beautiful gift. I also recommend these types of rituals to people who are just recognising they are an empath, as it has similar benefits while they learn to manage it from within.

Nowadays, I don't practice any of these rituals for myself at all. I simply don't feel the need to.

Over time, I've realised that simply *knowing* and *trusting* that I'm always protected is enough in itself. I also read tarot, am a medium and channel spirit regularly, and again, without practicing any of these protection rituals. I have never had an issue because I simply *know* that I am safe. I no longer allow fear to play a part – which in my opinion, is the mindset that opens you up to attracting the negativity you need protection from in the first place.

There are likely many, many parents out there who can completely relate to what I'm describing, and I want you to know that you're not alone; and you're certainly not crazy (even though at times, it may feel that way)! Being an empath can be challenging and confusing at the best of times, but when you're a parent as well, and don't know how to manage this gift, your heart and mind can get quite messy indeed. I can assure you that once you have the awareness, and the tools to effectively manage everything that being an empath entails, you will quickly realise just how very special a gift it is, and why you've been blessed with it. It's not always easy, but neither is life really, and the rewards that come with this gift far outweigh the challenges.

Christie

Highly sensitive people are too often perceived as weaklings or damaged goods. To feel intensely is not a symptom of weakness, it is the trademark of the truly alive and compassionate. It is not the empath who is broken, it is society that has become dysfunctional and emotionally disabled. There is no shame in expressing your authentic feelings. Those who are at times described as being a 'hot mess' or having 'too many issues' are the very fabric of what keeps the dream alive for a more caring, humane world. Never be ashamed to let your tears shine a light in this world.

Anthon St. Maarten

Links

Belinda Hayes – The Spiritual Teacher

BEE FREE HEALING
www.beefreehealing.com.au
@beefreehealing

THE SPIRITUAL TEACHER
www.thespiritualteacher.com.au
@thespiritualteacherAU

CRYSTAL COURSES
www.crystalcourses.com.au

HEALING WORKSHOPS
www.healingworkshops.com.au

RSH EXPO (Redland Spiritual & Healing Expo)
www.rshexpo.com.au
rshexpo@gmail.com
@RSHExpo

Danielle Renee - Holistic Therapist - Writer
Dip. Holistic Healing, Dip. Shiatsu & Oriental Therapies

www.holistic-danielle.com

Dr. Dawn Karima PhD

A conversation with Dawn Karima (radio show):
www.talktainmentradio.com/shows/conversationwithdawnkarima.html

The Desire of Nations (CD):
www.cdbaby.com/honeydawnkarima

The Stars of Heaven (CD):
www.cdbaby.com/dawnkarima

Jo Nicholls – Coach, Energy Worker & Therapist

www.thecrystalsanctuary.webs.com

www.facebook.com/Crystal.Sanctuary

Sharon Miralles – Energy Healer, Spiritual Teacher & Author

www.lightdivinehealings.com

www.facebook.com/pg/LightDivineHealings

Sheryl A. Stradling – Author

www.sherylstradling.com

Tracey Farrelly – Psychic Medium

www.angelsnbeyond.com.au

Christie Lyons – Lightworker, Publisher, Writer

www.whitelightpublishing.com.au

www.facebook.com/whitelightpublishing

Self Help Exercises

Danielle Renee – Holistic Therapist, Writer

Following are some self-help exercises that you might like to use to assist in keeping your auric energy field and your physical body in balance, especially if you find you are feeling emotional or taking on emotions of others.

Please note that the following techniques do not substitute medical, psychiatric, or psychological advice. You are strongly advised to consult your health care advisors about any medical concerns. Anyone using information shared by myself does so entirely at their own risk.

Bath Recipes
Having a bath assists in removing the emotions that are stored within our auras.

You can have a bath with a clear quartz crystal in it. Or, under a running tap you can pour a handful of Epsom salts, 3-4 drops of lavender oil and about a ¼ cup of apple cider vinegar. Have the temperature of the bath as hot as you can, without scolding yourself. Ensure that you drink a lot of water before and after the bath, as this is a detoxifying bath.

Grounding Meditation
When we are feeling overwhelmed with emotion, a grounding exercise can assist to bring yourself back

to connecting with the earth, rather than being in your head and feeling overwhelmed. This is a short exercise which you can do at the start of the end of your day.

Sit quietly in a chair with your feet firmly on the ground. Take in three deep breaths. Breathe in through your nose, and then out through your mouth. Slowly breathing in and out, take your awareness to your feet. Feel your feet connected to the ground. Sit and stay connected to the earth - breathing and feeling the earth supporting you under your feet. You can visualise roots from your feet growing down into the earth. Sit for five or ten minutes, staying connected to the earth.

Protection Exercise:
At the start of your day after completing the grounding exercise, visualise yourself in a protective bubble. Your bubble can be white or gold, or another colour that pops into your mind. Ask Source, God, Jesus or Archangel Michael to protect you throughout the day.

A process for identifying emotions felt (which is yours and which is someone else's, and healing this emotion):

Sit quietly in a chair with your feet firmly on the ground. Take in three deep breaths. Breathe in through your nose, and out through your mouth. Breathing normally, sit and feel into your emotions. When you feel an emotion, connect with it, feel it. Ask yourself, "Is this emotion mine or someone else's?" An answer will come to you. You may hear it as a voice, a thought or just a knowing of the answer. If the answer is yes, it is your own. Sit and ask God, Jesus or an Angel for it to be healed.

If it is someone else's emotion, ask for it to be removed from your body and energy field by saying "Please remove this emotion that is not mine". Ask source, God, Jesus or the Angels for the emotion to be transmuted in the violet flame. If you are unsure what you are feeling, or whether it is yours or not, ask for the emotion you are experiencing to be healed.

Burning Incense or Smudge Stick
I will often burn incense in my home to clear unwanted energies. I find incense balances the mind and body and dissolves any emotions. The smoke clears the aura and releases any negative or unwanted energies and assists to release any emotions that are not our own.

You can also purchase a white sage smudge stick. White sage is a cleanser, removing any negativity or stuck energy. You can burn this and walk around your home from room to room, wafting the smoke through the air. It is important to waft the smoke into each corner of the room you are in.

You can also waft the smoke around your entire body. Sit the sage stick in a flame or heat resistant container and using your hands, waft the smoke from head to toe. Whilst doing this, you can say to yourself "I now release and clear all negative thoughts and energy from my body and auric field".

I'm here to remind you, and myself, that all your feelings are welcome. All your emotions, your 'too much-ness', your intensity. All the parts of you that are deep and dark and challenging and hard.

They are welcome. They are beautiful and true. They are healing and powerful. They are the place from which the light is born. They are the reason you can feel so much love and joy.

Stephenie Zamora

An Empath

Being born an empath
Is certainly no easy feat
At times, it's such a struggle
With feelings you just can't beat

It's considered to be a blessing
Yet, can also be a curse
Feeling the energy of others
Is not always better, but worse

You can share in the joy of others
But also experience their pain
At times, you feel so elated
And at others, you feel so drained

It can be so exhausting
And tiring to say the least
But it also has its good points
For which upon you should feast

Sharing the feel-good emotions
Of love, compassion and joy
Being able to help heal others
Now, that is what I enjoy

You have a heightened sensitivity
To crowds, noise, light and the like
Which sometimes isn't easy
And what I most dislike

Unless you are an empath
It is hard to understand
The many emotions you go through
And the demand that it commands

You need a lot of alone time
To rejuvenate the soul
It can cause you to be a hermit at times
And retreat into a hole

You have to learn ways to protect yourself
And shield your auric fields
You really need to nurture your soul
Then you will see just what this yields

It's vital you set boundaries
So people don't abuse your good will
And when at times, you feel chaotic
It's important to just be still

But, all in all it's a blessing
It's also considered a gift
To be able to feel so strongly
Your intuition is never adrift

Empaths need more understanding
Of our sensitivity to all
All we really care to do
Is be kind, at peace, and loving to all.

Ros Sharp

Also available

White Light
PUBLISHING HOUSE